Christmas with Victoria

2003

Text by
Jennifer Ciegelski

Oxmoor
House®

HEARST COMMUNICATIONS, INC.

Oxmoor House, Inc.
Book Division of Southern Progress Corporation
P.O. Box 2463, Birmingham, AL 35201

ISBN: 0-8487-2737-1
ISSN: 1093-7633

Printed in Singapore
First printing 2003

We're here for you!
We at Oxmoor House are dedicated to serving you with reliable
information that expands your imagination and enriches your life.
We welcome your comments and suggestions. Please write us at:
Oxmoor House, Inc.
Christmas with Victoria
2100 Lakeshore Drive
Birmingham, AL 35209
To order additional publications, call (205) 445-6560 or visit us at
www.oxmoorhouse.com

For *Victoria* Magazine
Editor in Chief: Margaret Kennedy
Creative Director: Cynthia Hall Searight
www.victoriamag.com

Editor: John Smallwood
Designer: Curtis Potter

Produced by Smallwood & Stewart, Inc., New York City

Contents

For all the changes happening around us, there's something especially reassuring about tradition and ritual, and no more so than at Christmas. I take great pleasure and comfort in doing much the same thing every year: catching up with friends through cards and letters, decorating the house with precious ornaments that have been hidden away for months, gathering my extended family for dinners that revolve around treasured recipes.

And yet, at the same time, one of my greatest holiday delights is reinterpreting those very traditions and rituals. For me, finding new ways to keep the wonder and magic of the season alive can be as simple as wrapping my presents with special papers and ribbons, or choosing all new colors for the tree and table decorations, or designing and making my own place cards and gift tags.

Victoria Christmas is filled with just such ideas to keep your holiday traditions fresh and personal and always magical. It's all much easier than you might think. Join us on these pages, and we'll show you how.

Peggy Kennedy

Editor in Chief, *Victoria*

chapter 1

Inspired by Nature

Natural Wrappings
Ornaments from Nature
A Garden Indoors
Rethinking Wreaths
Dried Flowers and Pods
Giftsto the Gardener

Wherever the season may find you—surrounded by snow at an old country house or woodsy cabin, basking in the sun at a seaside cottage, or even in a city apartment—why not look to the boundless colors, shapes, and textures of nature for your holiday decor? Designs drawn from nature

enliven a home at any time of year, but most especially in midwinter. Winter greenery can take many forms beyond beloved holly and pine and fir Christmas trees, garlands, and wreaths—consider using miniature potted trees and plants; fragrant clippings of eucalyptus, boxwood or bay leaves; or fresh herbs such as rosemary and thyme. Branches of orange bittersweet or pink pepperberry add accents of color; various twigs, barks, and vines offer rustic charm. With a little paint or snips of twine, pods and pinecones and shells you may have collected throughout the year are transformed into ornaments that will hold their own against traditional glass decorations.

Unstructured beauty In nature, nothing is perfect, so decorate with a free hand. A simple wreath of cedar and seeded eucalyptus (opposite) presides above a mantel. Scallop shells underneath a cloche and a dangling starfish (above) are mementos from a vacation. Preceding pages: A clam basket is filled with starfish varieties and loops of natural cord awaiting their metamorphosis into ornaments for the tree. The table is laid with the same mix of greenery used on the mantel.

seaside celebration

Gifts of the deep Celebrate in a palette of sea blues and decorations inspired by underwater treasures. To dress each place setting, make instant napkin rings (left) by gluing scallop shells onto twine and tucking in a sprig of bay leaves. Better than coins in your stocking or a single Christmas star are these genuine sand dollars and dried starfish (below), their bleached-out color a wonderful take on winter white. Try inking them and hand-printing patterns on plain butcher paper to make your own gift wrap, or paint them gold or silver and hang them on the tree with twine. Sprigs of fragrant eucalyptus and bay leaves extend beyond the mantel and join seashells to decorate window ledges (opposite).

Artful gift wrap creates excitement about the secrets within

natural wrappings

When your holiday decor draws its theme from nature, gifts wrapped in brightly colored papers tied with shiny satin ribbons tend to look out of place. A softer palette, and softer material, are better choices. **Papers** A visit to a fine stationery store will uncover a variety of handmade wrapping papers textured by fibers, leaves, and flower petals (opposite, top left). Or you can make your own papers using appliquéd pressed flowers or inked imprints of leaves, seashells or bark. Wide rolls of brown kraft paper or white butcher's paper provide the perfect canvas. **Toppers** Like a star on the tip of the tree, a topper is something no gift should be without. Nature's idea of a good one might include a seashell (opposite, top right); a pinecone, a sprig of holly, herbs, or other greenery; even a walnut adhered with a knot or a bit of glue. **Ties** In lieu of fancy colored ribbons or metallic cords, secure your packages with yardage in more unusual choices such as raffia, twine (gardener's, butcher's, or waxed varieties), rickrack, colored yarn, twill hem tape, seam binding, and thin rope (opposite, bottom left). **Tags** Use leftover materials—even scraps of corrugated cardboard—to design your own gift tags and greeting cards. Embellish the papers with sprigs of winter greenery (opposite, bottom right), shells, berries, twigs, or pressed flowers in keeping with your theme.

Natural Selections

Borrow these palettes and accents from nature for your gifts.

Garden Combine greens with pastel yellow or pink yarn and add silk or crepe paper flowers, velvet leaves, paper insects.

Harvest Use deep red and gold hues embellished with wheat stalks, dried gourds, rough twines, or grapevines.

Seaside Choose a spectrum of blues and sandy shades dotted with shells, sand dollars, starfish, bits of driftwood, and twine.

Woodland Stay with a palette of dark greens and browns accented with pinecones, birch bark, hollies, cinnamon sticks, and sprigs of bittersweet.

Magical transformation With a little imagination (and some white paint), backyard or forest finds become delightful decorations. A spiraling wisteria pod turns into an icicle (right), while a pinecone, an acorn, and milkweed pods join to form an angel trumpeting a song on high (below). Learn how to make a Pinecone Angel for your tree on page 134.

Naturally adorned A tree trimmed in natural ornaments has an understated elegance that one decorated with store-bought decorations rarely has. This stunning study in white and gold (opposite) mixes classics such as blown-glass balls and teardrops with handmade wisteria-pod icicles, pinecone angels, painted leaves, and starbursts made from sweet-gum balls injected with dozens of toothpick rays. Beneath the tree are piles of gifts wrapped with handmade papers containing leaves and sprigs of greenery alongside twisty brown orbs hand-woven from Virginia creeper.

ornaments from nature

Growing concerns Devoted gardeners need not feel blue at the end of the growing season. There are plenty of activities to undertake indoors that will satisfy all green-thumbed urges. A sunny window is an ideal spot to establish an indoor garden (opposite). Outdoor ornaments such as statuary and gazing balls that might be forgotten in the snow and ice can watch over plants and bulbs inside. Gather pods and seeds throughout the season for holiday projects like this handsome Nut Topiary (right) dotted with dried rose hips and hazelnuts. You'll find the instructions to make the topiary on page 135.

Forcing bulbs

Flower bulbs are marvelously engineered to survive in the frozen earth through the winter. With a little work you can trick their inner timing mechanism into sending out beautiful flowers ahead of schedule to brighten any corner during the holidays.

Amaryllis and paperwhite narcissus are forcing favorites, because they don't require a period of chilling before planting. Hyacinth, tulips, and daffodils need to be kept cold for a time in order to simulate the winter; if you're an exerienced gardener you can cool them yourself, although it's much simpler to buy "pre-cooled" bulbs. If you buy and plant in mid- to late fall the bulbs should be in bloom by Christmas. The planting procedure is the same for all, although details like the size of the pot will change according to variety.

Arrange the bulbs in a well-drained pot with two inches of soil, or a watertight container with two inches of gravel, then add more soil or gravel to come up to the top of the bulbs. Plant very close together for the best display. Don't worry about overcrowding, as a tightly-packed pot will make a dazzling display when the flowers are out. Keep the container in a cool place until shoots begin to show, then transfer to a warmer spot where the bulbs will get indirect light.

After they begin to flower, it's best to remove the bulbs from direct light so they stay in bloom longer. If your bulbs bud too early, the process can be slowed by moving pots to a cool, dark place.

rethinking wreaths

Even the plainest cedar or pine wreath can be made exciting. Weave in other greens such as ivy and holly to give it more visual flair and add sprigs of bittersweet or other berries for color. A few dried roses or hydrangeas will also add variety. The simple holiday wreath can be rethought in dozens of ways. Shape Recall your principles of geometry to form a square wreath like this one made of long-lasting Spanish apple surrounding a mirror (opposite, top left), or try an oval, a triangle, or whatever shape suits your fancy. Color While green might be the first color that pops into your mind, it's not the only one. A fresh or dried wreath in an unexpected hue such as a brilliant red (opposite, top right) preserves the feeling of the season and catches the eye anywhere it is placed. Think of amaranth, bittersweet, winterberry, or pepperberry as colorful options. Components Don't stop at greenery clippings—a wreath composed of objects such as pinecones (opposite, bottom left), jingle bells, glass ornament balls, millinery fruit, or velvet leaves is equally festive. Fragrance Evergreen and pine are fragrant symbols of Yuletide, but herbs such as rosemary (opposite, bottom right) and fresh eucalyptus are delightful alternatives to scent your home.

Sturdy Foundations

It's quite simple to make a wreath, especially when you have a good form as a base. Here are the most basic styles available at crafts stores:

Foam A lightweight base on which to glue beads, candies, or ornaments. Florist's foam can be soaked in water and used as a base for a live flower arrangement.

Straw Provides a full, rounded base to which organic elements such as leaves, dried flowers, nuts, and pinecones can easily be pinned or glued.

Wire Designed to be a sturdy enough support for heavy clippings such as evergreens, which are wired to the base. Available in single-wire (for thin wreaths) or double-wire (for lush wreaths).

A wreath's beauty may be fresh and fleeting or dry and everlasting

Layered approach The mantel is a virtual stage for a dioramic fantasy of greenery and flowers during the holidays. While you can layer the greenery as much as you like, one dominant element should stand out. For this rustic brick hearth (opposite), an urn is filled with a wild assortment of cut greens. Red winterberries and an amaryllis provide bright accents of secondary color, and additional branches and beloved objects such as a bee skep, a moss obelisk, lotus pods, and vine orbs fill out the mantel shelf. Below, a colorful mix of red, orange, and gold roses is accented with pinecones, juniper cuttings, and rosehips. The architecture of the mantel is underscored with a fringe of leaves; you may try a similar lineup using galax, lemon, or magnolia leaves.

lush assemblages

Fruits and foliage Instead of fresh flowers, use the colors and textures of fresh and dried fruit to enliven seasonal foliage. An arrangement in a large urn (right) juxtaposes evergreen cuttings with lady apples, dried orange slices, hypericum berries, and some vivid red dahlias. If you don't have the time or the inclination to create layers on the mantel, a singular arrangement like this one is a stunning substitute—and easy to clean up once Christmas has passed. Don't have a fireplace to decorate? No room for a full-size tree? An elegant tabletop topiary (below) will provide a focus for holiday cheer in a different way. This one is built on a base of live ivy and is dotted with lady apples, orange Chinese lanterns, bicolor roses, and viburnum berries.

fruitful additions

Graced with vines Needing little arrangement to look good, vines, twigs (opposite), and berried branches such as bittersweet, winterberry, and holly can be used to introduce lacy, natural forms thoughout the house. Try twining vines around a banister, a chandelier, table legs, or the back of a wooden chair or drape them around doorways or windows. This unusual sconce (below), created from an old wirework frame and a dish of beeswax candles, is dressed for the holidays with strands of bittersweet.

branches and vines

dried flowers and pods

It's a myth that the beauty of the garden is fleeting. There are many varieties of flowers and plants that can be dried and preserved and used in holiday decorating projects in the deepest days of winter. Here are a few of our favorites. Swags A variation on the wreath and garland, swags are lovely, indoors or out, at the corners of a window or doorway. This version (opposite, top left) features branches, herbs, and eucalyptus punctuated with the soft, dusty pink of dried garden roses and a cluster of pepperberry. Kissing balls As the name implies, this spherical decoration (opposite, top right) is often hung in doorways in lieu of mistletoe as a place to steal a kiss. It's easy to make with several dozen dried rosebuds secured in a foam ball. Simply hang it from a pretty ribbon. Garlands Use fresh greenery to provide the base for a garland, and add natural dried elements for texture and color. This harvest-themed version (opposite, bottom left) has accents of dried gourds, oak leaves, wheat sheaves, and ponderosa pinecones. A second garland of drilled and strung nuts is draped over it. Gift accents A dried flower, cinnamon sticks, or nuts are enchanting toppers on a gift. If you don't have a perfect dried specimen but would still like that natural look, try to find faux designs crafted out of fiber or paper, like this magnolia blossom (opposite, bottom right).

Drying Methods

Collect elements from your garden all year to use in your holiday decorating and dry them in a cool, well-ventilated place, such as a potting shed or garage, for several weeks.

Flowers Harvest roses, hydrangeas, lavender, and other flowers when they aren't damp from rain or dew. Hang them upside down so they dry straight.

Gourds Wipe clean of soil or any garden debris and dry on sheets of newspaper. To use, just drill a small hole through the neck.

Leaves Oak, maple, and magnolia leaves all preserve beautifully. For best results, layer between sheets of newspaper and press under a stack of books.

Pods Hang lotus pods, nigella, thistles, Chinese lanterns, silver dollars, and other everlastings upside down from their stems.

At their peak, dried flowers and pods become spectacular ornaments

Natural imagery Any green thumb will be delighted by the gift of botanical prints of favorite plants (right) or a vintage garden book. Often full of exquisite engravings, sketches, and color illustrations, old garden volumes (opposite) are artistic treasures. Wrap these gifts simply in translucent glassine paper or green florist's tissue so decorative images show through, then tie with florist's twine.

Gifts for gardeners

Gardening is such a popular pastime that there are plenty of themed gifts you can select and create.

Flower press Encourage the preservation of favorite blooms with this thoughtful tool. Include a blank scrapbook to store the pressings.

Heirloom seeds Seed exchanges nationwide now source hard-to-find seeds for heirloom varieties. Sign up a friend for a membership, or create a personalized set of seeds for her or him to try.

Journal Every gardener needs a permanent place to record planting schemes and seasonal changes. Choose a beautiful blank book and inscribe the recipient's name on the flyleaf.

Forcing kit Gather some forceable bulbs (try amaryllis, narcissus, or hyacinth) along with a special vase designed for forcing (or a glass dish at least 3 inches high on the sides with stones for the roots to take hold). Place in a brown bag and tie with twine. See page 21 for more detailed forcing instructions.

Gloves and boots Odds are that every serious gardener either loses or wears out his or her gloves every season. Treat your friend to a brand-new pair, along with some colorful rubber garden boots or shoes.

Timeless treasures Search flea market or antiques shops for garden-themed gifts: colorful vintage seed packets for framing, old watering cans or florist's frogs for flower arrangements.

chapter 2

*The Gift
of Giving*

VELVET-CUFFED STOCKINGS
PATTERNS FROM THE PAST
GRAPHIC WRAPS
CLEVER CONTAINERS
FRAMED MEMORIES
RIBBON PORTRAITS
FRAGRANT SACHETS

*T*winkling ornaments aside, everyone knows that the true spirit of Christmas resides in giving. For some, this means giving of time, or sumptuous dinners and treats from the kitchen. For others, giving manifests itself in thoughtful presents to delight loved ones. Whatever the gift, the sentiment you express is the same—you are showing how much you care. But to make something really meaningful, get personal. Add an embroidered monogram to a set of napkins, frame a photograph of a pet, fill a stocking with spices and spoons for a cook, hand tools and seeds for a gardener or bookplates and bookmarks for a bibliophile. If you have the time, make gifts by hand or create your own wrappings or personalized gift tags. On the following pages we've assembled inventive projects and wrapping ideas that even a novice can master. So gather your materials and bring a personal touch to all your gifts.

Stylish stockings They're usually filled with smaller presents, but stockings are a handsome gift on their own. They're simple to sew, and can be made with fabric and trims from other projects, from sophisticated velvet-cuffed toile (opposite), to traditional plaid and herringbone (above). Instructions are on page 136. Preceding pages: Christmas is a time for visiting friends, and a box of ornaments makes a lovely hostess gift. As a welcoming touch for guests, leave presents for Christmas morning in their room.

patterned papers

Patterns from the past The elegant script of old handwritten documents makes for captivating wrapping paper with some simple photocopying. Letters, postcards, ledgers, recipe cards, or sheet music found at flea markets and antiques stores, or your own sketches can be turned into wrappable art. Even vintage wallpaper or fabric swatches can be "repurposed" in this way (below). For an old-fashioned touch, tear the edges of the photocopied papers and use sealing wax (left) or decoupage snippets and found images to dress up a simple giftbox (opposite). Instructions for making a decoupage box are on page 137.

Paper palettes The patterns may vary widely but choosing gift wrap in coordinating colors creates a unified look underneath your tree. For these grown-up presents (opposite and right), chic black and white are all over—in wide stripes, polka dots, harlequin diamonds, and handcrafted handwriting designs created on a photocopier. Accent colors of vibrant green and yellow on the satin ribbons and tags take their cue from the ornaments on the lovably straggly tree.

Scheming in color

Keeping seasonal color combinations simple is a reliable formula for success—especially on the tree, where too many colors can cancel each other out. When in doubt, keep to a single color—say gold or silver for the tree—then use a contrasting palette for all your gift wrap and ribbons. Here are some alternative pairings to traditional red and green.

Black & White If you're creating your own papers, look to the graphic appeal of dominos, playing cards, toile, etchings, stripes, and checkerboards as inspiration. Keep things lively by using ribbons or gift tags in accent colors of hot pink or red, citrusy greens, yellows, and oranges, or silver and gold.

Blue, Silver & White At this time of year, the world outside clothes itself in icy winter hues. Let the frosty colors of twilight skies, stars, icicles, and snowflakes inspire your choices of colors and patterns for wrappings and decorations.

Ivory & Gold You may already have ivory and gold elements in your decorating scheme in the way of serving pieces and vases; play them up for the holidays, or enhance their innately dressy quality with subtle touches of red and green.

Pink & Pistachio This pairing is an updated, feminine interpretation of the more traditional red and green of the season—and softer on the eye.

clever containers

Christmas cones The concept of the favor cone dates back to Victorian times. These days, such nostalgic receptacles are perfect for small gifts or edible treats. Dangling from a branch on a Christmas tree (left) or sharing space with other ornaments in a pretty compote (opposite), they are decorative, too. Paper cones like the vintage-themed ones at left are simple to make. You can embellish them with cutouts of found images or photocopies of illustrations from vintage cards or children's books. The rose cone was simply made from a photocopy of a ladies' handkerchief. Turn to page 138 for the instructions.

Glamorous gift bags As the holiday party tempo picks up, a gift of wine or spirits for your host may be just the thing to keep the celebration going. Bottles can be awkward to wrap with paper, so a more beautiful (and reusable) option to conceal your gift would be a fabric bag (right) tied with a ribbon or tasseled cording. With basic sewing skills, you can make your own; you'll find instructions on page 139.

framed memories

Stumped by what to give the person in your life who has "everything?" Here's an idea: Find an object that has some special meaning to her—a piece of vintage fabric that she's always loved, perhaps, or an old postcard that recalls a childhood vacation—and frame it in a beautiful shadow-box. You may find ideas and inspiration from the following themes: ANTIQUE LINENS Often forgotten in a drawer or stored away in an attic, hand towels and handkerchiefs with embroidered monograms are works of art (opposite, top left). MINIATURE COLLECTIONS Seemingly mundane objects such as keys and carved buttons (opposite, top right) are imbued with new life when arranged in a collage-style series. Household odds and ends, garden seed packets, and vintage labels are other possibilities. SYMBOLIC TOKENS A single three-dimensional item makes a statement. An old silver spoon (opposite, bottom left) may be a fitting gift for a friend who frequently entertains; a baby's shoe or mitten would be a touching keepsake for a new mother. UNUSUAL FINDS think of turning cherished flea market finds that serve no practical purpose into something sculptural in their own right—this gentleman's collar (opposite, bottom right), for example, which arcs artistically inside a frame.

Shadow-box Tips

Consider the elements when choosing a shadow-box.

Frame style Select a frame to complement the object. Its materials should help guide the overall feeling—a frame of wood veneer or gilded silver or gold projects a different mood from one of weathered wood or painted wire.

Background matting For simple objects, a patterned damask fabric or a marbleized paper works well; for a decorative piece, textured parchment paper or neutral-colored linen would be a better backdrop.

Glass covering Ultraviolet glass or an archival-quality synthetic covering helps protect fragile objects such as printed postcards, photographs, or fabrics that may fade in sunlight.

Frame an object and you capture a memory to treasure

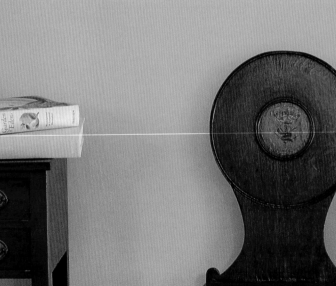

Gallery gift Creating an art gallery (opposite) for a friend is easier than it may seem—the "artworks" are color photocopies from books and the "frames" are ribbon. Scour used bookstores for volumes of interest (right), then photocopy the images on sturdy paper. Choose brocaded, embroidered, and ruched ribbons in colors to complement the art. A steady hand and some fabric glue is all it takes to create the borders. For added durability, mount the prints on foam-core board before applying the ribbon.

Suitable for framing

Flea markets, used book stores, and tag sales are good sources for old prints, postcards, and magazines to turn into framed gifts.

Animal books Look for biology classifications or prints by masters such as Audubon. Try varied images of a single animal—dogs, birds, fish, or butterflies.

Architectural drawings Renderings of famous buildings make a lovely series, as do classical elements such as columns, pediments, and statuary.

Botanicals Peruse out-of-print garden books or horticultural manuals for frameable images of flowers, leaves, trees, herbs, fruits, and vegetables.

Images for kids Create framed art for a child you know with illustrations and text from vintage books of nursery rhymes, ABCs, or fairy tales.

Fabric patterns Photocopy interesting fabric swatches or even colorful vintage scarves or antique ladies' handkerchiefs.

Fashion illustrations Check out fashion magazines from the early twentieth century to find charming drawings of the looks of the day.

Maps Even an armchair traveler would appreciate a collection made from old school atlases, travel guides, and road maps of favorite destinations.

well-loved decorations

Past perfect Some of the most heartwarming gifts and decorations are vintage classics, made by hand in a whimsical, primitive style. Don't overlook these beauties when rummaging through flea markets and tag sales, and be sure they're passed along to good homes where their time-worn beauty will be appreciated. Here, a hand-painted snowman sign (above) and a jointed Santa toy (right) serve yet another year on their new owner's Christmas tree.

Soothing scents A tiny scented sachet will sweeten a closet or drawer. Dried flowers, potpourri and other materials can be purchased ready-made, or you can dry and mix favorites yourself. Popular choices include lavender buds, rose petals, heather, jasmine, and cedar needles. Leave flowers, leaves and spices whole; break up bark and roots into small pieces. A few drops of an essential oil—rose, lavender, orange, pine—will strengthen the scent. Mix the materials and store in sealed glass jars for six weeks to allow the fragrances to mingle and deepen. Sew three sides of the pouches together, then add your mixture and sew up the last side. Package three sachets in a little stack secured with ribbon or twine and a gift tag. For pretty pillow-shaped versions (opposite and above), we chose muslin with an airy weave (to let the perfume through) and classic ticking stripes, but feel free to work with whatever fabric scraps you have on hand.

fragrant sachets

chapter 3

Magical Touches

Mantel Finery
Timeless Treasures
Window Wonders
The Essence of Holiday Sparkle
Precious Still Lifes

Christmas is a time to decorate with abandon. Passionate collectors of holiday ephemera rediscover their treasures each December with glee, but even the most reserved among us can't resist the urge to deck our halls with special tokens of the season. Let your boughs be laden with ornaments in

Holiday hues Sophisticates might fancy metallics (opposite), and elegant arrangements in silver, bronze, and gold. For traditionalists, Christmas wouldn't be the same without red and green. There are always new ways to use them—to infuse ordinary glass vases with holiday red, simply fill them with cranberries (above) or colored marbles. Preceding pages: Ornaments resembling sugared fruits are just a few of the gems on a life-size feather tree spilling over with treasures.

a multitude of sizes, shapes, and colors. Dress every mantel with an enchanting mix of greenery, flora, and a few little surprises to admire while you sit by the fire. Compose a colorful tabletop still life inspired by your favorite collection. Create the illusion of icicles indoors with an assortment of sparkly ornaments hanging in a window. If there's no room on the tree, fill glass bowls or vases with surplus ornaments and place them on window ledges, bedside tables, or in entrance halls. Drape swags of colored glass beads around mirrors or windows. Through these decorations, displayed with affection and care, we create lasting memories for our friends and family to treasure and beloved traditions we welcome year after year.

mantel finery

Natural hearthscapes The mantel is second only to the tree as the focal point for holiday decorations. For harmony, choose a unified color scheme for both. Flanked by winter-white floral arrangements and dressed with boxwood, an architectural mirror (left) reflects flickers of mercury glass votives and silver candlesticks. A rustic stone hearth (below) sets a stage for a rhythmic march of diminutive evergreens and red roses interlaced with cranberry garlands. An unadorned magnolia wreath (opposite) strikes a woodsy tone of muted browns and greens. Decorative pairs of hurricane lamps and pinecone wreaths bring a pleasing symmetry to the mantel composition.

timeless treasures

Collecting old-fashioned ornaments for the tree can be a year-round pastime, whether you seek newly minted baubles or vintage examples. For added interest, chose a theme to guide your hunt; here are a few of our favorites.

FIGURES & FAUNA Ornaments modeled after St. Nick are, of course, a given, but you might also look for other characters of the season including snowmen, polar bears, reindeer, and angels (opposite, top left). DESTINATIONS & LANDMARKS Travelers of both the real and armchair varieties are charmed by souvenirs of buildings and icons from around the world—how about a clock tower or windmill (opposite, top right) bobbing from the branches of your tree? CHILDREN & TOYS It's no surprise that ornaments in the shape of hobby horses, drums, alphabet blocks, nursery-rhyme characters, and even children themselves (opposite, bottom left) are so popular, especially with kids. FRUITS & VEGETABLES Some of the earliest European blown-glass ornaments imitated the bounty that families hoped to reap throughout the year. New and old ornaments in the form of fruit baskets (opposite, bottom right) and cornucopias, as well as oranges, apples, bunches of grapes and nuts, are all readily available.

Vintage Collectibles

Be on the lookout for pieces of holiday history at tag sales and antiques stores.

Dresdens Made from the 1880s until World War I, these hand-painted, gilded, embossed cardboard decorations were once very popular but are now rare. Three-dimensional versions probably held candy.

Feather trees Made from goose or chicken feathers, originals from the 1890s to the 1940s are rare; a few companies now produce similar trees.

Kugels Introduced to the United States from Germany around 1880, these silvered glass orbs quickly became very popular. Larger versions were probably intended to hang in windows or doorways.

Lametta Silvery tinsellike tufts on a flexible wire base were fashioned into garlands and ornaments. Old pieces are very fragile but have a lovely tarnished patina.

New and old become beloved heirlooms

Light fantastic If the tree overflows with ornaments, send extras to the windows, where they can glimmer like indoor icicles. Those made of colored glass, crystal, or mirrors will catch the bright-white light reflected on the snow outside. Even droplets from a chandelier or beaded strands from a glass necklace can be used to shimmering effect. Thread the ornaments securely with snippets of ribbon or metallic cording tied to a curtain rod, and remember to stagger their lengths so as to help prevent collisions.

window wonders

Magical mirrors Like a sleight-of-hand artist, you can play many tricks with mirrors. Add one or several to a room decked in holiday finery and everything is instantly multiplied and more festive. Use mirrors' reflective powers to enhance the shimmering intensities of candlelight, as this peephole mirror does with tall tapers and votives (right). Hanging small looking glasses as if they were art (opposite)—especially when the frames themselves are artful—is a wonderful way to dress up a plain space. Choose complementary sizes and styles (these are all gold-leafed) and securely attach them to wide ribbons.

The essence of holiday sparkle

Looking for a way to light up gray days and chilly evenings? Even without a roaring fire, here are easy ideas for adding a little magic to your home.

Candles Votives, pillars, and tapers are inexpensive ways to create a warm, intimate environment filled with soft, ever-changing light. To create instant atmosphere, dim the electric lights, then group candles generously, or put out singles to enliven dark hallways, powder rooms, and other unexpected places.

Crystal Now is the time to bring all your best pieces out of hiding. Crystal candlesticks and goblets call to mind winter's ice. Pile blown-glass globe ornaments into bowls and compotes.

Mercury glass While true mercury is no longer used, modern reproductions abound in silver and metallic colors. Look for candleholders, serving pieces, and butler's balls to highlight your tables and mantels.

Mirrors Propped on a living room mantel or hung above a dining room buffet, full-size mirrors reflect the energy around them tenfold. Lay smaller mirrors flat on a tabletop and place flickering votives or seasonal arrangements on top to multiply their effect.

Silver With company coming, by all means polish up your good silver and put it out on display. Candelabras, julep cups, coffee sets, and serving pieces lend instant glamour to casual and formal celebrations alike.

precious still lifes

For a truly personalized twist on holiday decorating, consider surrounding yourself with a show-and-tell of the things you love. Your collection need not be lavish or even expensive; just try to make sure the palette or the overall design of the objects contributes to the merriment in your home. FESTIVE PATTERNS A good pattern adds a jaunty note to a room. If you're lucky enough to have several pieces of tartanware (opposite, top left), you know that its red and green colors seamlessly meld with traditional holiday decor. Items with polka dots or multicolored stripes would also be effective accents. SPARKLING JEWEL-TONES Garnet, emerald, sapphire, amethyst—colors borrowed from gemstones lend unique richness. One source might be etched-glass or cut-crystal vases, decanters, or goblets (opposite, top right). SHIMMERING METALLICS The luster of silvered or colored mercury glass catches and reflects light beautifully. The vases, candlesticks, and gazing balls in this grouping (opposite, bottom left) date from between 1860 and 1920. COLORFUL IMAGERY Collectors may flaunt a full service on the table for Christmas dinner, but unused tureens and odd platters and teacups in floral or architectural themes are lovely in their own right. This collection is mostly English Staffordshire (opposite, bottom right).

Ways to Display

Make your treasured collection the center of holiday attention; just be sure it's well out of harm's way.

Centerpieces Smaller collections are particularly suited to serve as conversation starters at the center of the dinner table. Delicate objects can be placed on a pedestal cake stand to keep them above the action.

End tables A dim hallway, dark nook, or lonely corner is instantly brightened by the addition of a small (but sturdy) end table piled high with colorful crystal serveware, a bowl of blown-glass Christmas ornaments, or a grouping of sterling silver.

Shelves Bookshelves, wall niches, windowed armoires, curio cabinets, and hutches help protect precious pieces while still keeping them on view for all to enjoy.

Cherished collections on view for the holiday show

Dining room dressing Dress up your dining area and tabletop with decorations in multiples: In this room (right), a coordinated series of objects works together to set a lovely scene. Why stop at one large wreath in the window when you can display several scaled-down ones? On the table (below), forgo a traditional solitary centerpiece and opt for a succession of smaller arrangements mingled with candles high and low.

numbers game

chapter 4

Gracious

Goodness

PRECIOUS PRESERVES
SWEET BITES
CONES OF COOKIES
SPICY SESAME SOY NUTS
CHOCOLATE DECADENCE

From the spicy scent of fresh-baked gingerbread cookies to the savory aroma of a roasted goose, the kitchen is the fragrant focal point of any holiday preparations. Why not make it a center for gift-giving as well? Luscious creations from your kitchen can be remarkably easy

to make and package, and they bear the warmest and most personal of greetings. For one- and two-bite treats such as cookies, chocolates, and candies, think in quantity: Don't even bother making a mere handful—beyond those you'll be giving as gifts, you'll no doubt be indulging in a few tastes yourself! Set aside a quiet afternoon, revisit favorite family recipes, and try the new ones you'll find in these pages. Your efforts in the kitchen are sure to find an appreciative audience, from the hostess of a Christmas cocktail party to a loved one far away. Select packaging suitable for the gift within—secured with colored ribbon, even everyday kitchen wrappings such as cellophane and fluted paper can get in the holiday spirit.

Jeweled jellies Jams and jellies sparkling in clear glass jars (opposite) are always welcome gifts. Try seasonal combinations such as Cranberry and Blood Orange Conserve (above), presented in a lacy Moroccan tea glass. Preceding pages: We've tucked a handful of Hazelnut Gems into a tiny tote, and poured a sampling of Herb and Cranberry Vinegars into crystal cruets. Turn to pages 132, 131, and 133 for the recipes.

sweet bites

Cookie cornucopias A cone is a perfect little holder for bite-size, buttery Christmas cookies (left). To make your own, simply twist and tape a square of heavy silver or gold paper into shape, then line it with wax paper. Finish by gluing on a snippet of cord or ribbon and a tiny ornament as a special Christmas keepsake.

Truffle favors No trifles, these truffles (opposite). When tucked into shimmering organza bags (lined with cellophane) and piled on top of a trio of cakestands, they become delectable gifts for guests. The dark-chocolate nuggets are perked with peppermint and lightly dusted with cocoa. Turn to page 128 for the recipe. Their live counterparts may be poky, but these chocolate caramel turtles (right) will practically scoot off the plate. For a hostess gift, include a pretty dish, such as this creamware one, to double the delight. Enclose in cellophane and tie with patterned ribbon. The recipe is on page 125.

Sweet and savory surprises
Adults who crave cookies will be thrilled to receive a grown-up take on their favorite treat. These sophisticated Chocolate Espresso Cookies (opposite) are doubly indulgent—the chocolate batter is intensified with espresso and chunks of bittersweet chocolate. Pack them carefully in cupcake papers in a colorful tin so they arrive intact at their destination. Turn to page 130 for the recipe. Nuts are as much a part of the holidays as cocoa and candy canes. For a spicy snack, Sesame Soy Nuts (right) have a delicious flavor that will ensure they won't last long. Turn to page 102 for the recipe.

Under Wraps

Bags Dress up plain brown paper bags with festive tags, ribbon, or holiday stickers, or create your own from fabric scraps cut with pinking shears and gathered together at the top with a brightly colored ribbon.

Baskets Baskets are ideal for gifts with multiple components. Assemble a kitchen basket of edible gifts and useful implements for a cook, for example, then line or wrap baskets with tea towels or pieces of fabric, or fill them with excelsior or shredded paper.

Boxes Cookies and candies are at home and safe in white bakery boxes, wooden boxes in different shapes, or even Chinese food containers. Embellish with greenery, glitter, or ink stamps.

Jars Decorate with a gummed label on the lid or front of the jar to let the recipient know what's inside. Cut a cap of fabric with pinking shears; hold it in place with ribbon or waxed twine.

Papers A smart choice for a range of edible goodies, especially buttery loaves or cakes. Choose from wax paper, parchment paper, or kraft or butcher's paper. Tie with colored string or patterned ribbon.

Tins Essential for keeping cookies and crackers crisp and chocolates and fudge fresh. Round tins in Christmas colors are classic, but don't overlook vintage versions you might find in an antiques store. Simply line them with a few folds of wax paper.

Chocolate choices Anything made with chocolate is always welcome. Studded with dried cherries, this Chocolate Brioche Loaf (below) may be light in texture but it is rich in flavor— a tantalizing tea loaf. You can substitute dried cranberries for a tangy seasonal flavor. To pattern the parchment paper wrapping, try a special paper punch, as we did, or an embosser. The cupcake "knots" of this festive Yule log, or Bûche de Noël (opposite), mimic a real tree. It's made like a layer cake; no rolling is required. The fun is sculpting icing along the edge to look like bark, the top as tree rings. Turn to pages 126 and 124 for the recipes.

WHITE CHRISTMAS

decadent delights

chapter 5

Holiday Dining

Good Beginnings
Table Graces
New Year's Supper
Sumptuous Side Dishes
Say Cheese

One of the best things about Christmas is the time we get to spend with those we love. Out-of-town relatives come in for a visit, and friends drop by for company and conversation. We welcome them all warmly into our homes, often to sit down together to share a holiday feast:

Good beginnings Welcome guests with a few savory nibbles that will stimulate their appetites, such as these Spicy Pecans and Miniature Caramelized Onion Tartlets (opposite); the recipes are on page 102 and 103. Warming Apple-Rutabaga Soup (above) dressed up with whipped cream is a delicious prelude to the main attraction; turn to page 104 for the recipe. Preceding pages: Our turkey is first soaked in a flavorful herbal brine, then roasted; the recipe is on page 112.

nourishment for all the senses as the comforting sounds and smells from the kitchen fill the house. This is the time to set a table as generous and rich and special as the food we're preparing. Select the linens, china, and silverware and plan the seating arrangement and decorations well in advance. If possible, get the table ready ahead of time—between cooking and attending to guests and family you may not have a lot of time on the day. Don't hold anything back—everything should speak of warmth and bounty and festive spirit. Layer your best linens for even greater effect, bring out your crystal; personalize each place setting with a different mix of seasonal greenery, small ornaments, and fresh fruit.

table graces

Starting with Thanksgiving dinner and continuing through a drowsy-but-jovial brunch on New Year's Day, the holiday table is the center of much activity and good cheer. And in the same way we decorate the tree for the season, we can dress the table for these occasions as well. DISHWARE If you have a set of fine china (opposite, top left)—a wedding gift, perhaps, or handed down from your grandparents—now is certainly the time to use and enjoy it. You might also look for interesting patterns at estate sales and assemble a mix-and-match table in a charming jumble of designs. Chargers, platters, and tureens can all be put to good use with your holiday menus. LINENS Tablecloths, runners, and napkins in Yuletide colors or patterns instantly put any table in the spirit. Accent each napkin with a special token (we used a mother-of-pearl buckle opposite, top right), a tiny ornament, or a few inches of ribbon or tasseled cording. GLASSWARE When you're ready to raise a toast with a fine vintage or some bubbly, set the table with special glassware (opposite, bottom left) such as flutes, goblets, and wine glasses in crystal, blown glass, or even colorful cut-glass designs. PLACE CARDS They may seem old-fashioned, but cards (opposite, bottom right) are an effective way to help guests find their seats easily, add another decorative element to the table, and enable the hostess to arrange for lively conversation.

Place Cards

Go beyond the standard tented card and show your guests to their seats with style.

Favors Attach place cards to a little something for guests to take home: a candy cane, a piece of marzipan or chocolate candy, a tiny ornament.

Holders Tuck place cards into decorative stands or tiny picture frames, or use small pine cones or lady apples as card stands.

Supplies While plenty of preprinted cards are readily available, you can easily make your own. Choose sturdy papers and embellish them with ink stamps or a picture of the guest. Cut with pinking shears, and handwrite the names in ink with a flourish.

A handmade place card is a thoughtful welcome

New Year's Supper

Pasta in Champagne Sauce
with Golden Caviar
Crown Roast of Lamb
Wild Rice Pilaf
Spiced Beet Medley

When only a special few are on the guest list for a sophisticated New Year's Eve celebration, choose a menu that raises simple dishes to sheer elegance. Our pasta with caviar is impressively luxurious, yet it's completely affordable and requires minimal effort to prepare. To make sure you're not too busy to join in the fun, set up a buffet with something special—we suggest a crown roast of lamb—as the dramatic centerpiece accompanied by savory side dishes with an unexpected twist. After dinner, serve a special dessert and pour cordials or Cognac while you reflect on the year that's passed.

A cozy gathering This New Year's Eve, start with something surprising but totally in keeping with the spirit of the occasion, such as Pasta in Champagne Sauce with Golden Caviar (above), recipe on page 111. Then move on to the meaty masterpiece, an impressive Crown Roast of Lamb stuffed with Wild Rice Pilaf (opposite), recipes are on pages 113 and 109. Serve the accompanying Spiced Beet Medley in a glass dish to put the glorious gold and ruby colors on display, recipe on page 106. Ready for another course? Go European style with a salad following the entree (left). This crispy concoction of mixed greens surprises the palate with slivers of aged goat cheese, chopped walnuts, and juicy pomegrante seeds.

choosing sides

Like supporting actors to a star, side dishes are often unsung heroes. Yet a holiday feast just wouldn't be the same without them. Whether you're cooking an entire meal at home or asked to bring along a dish to a dinner party, you'll want to prepare sides that add dimension to the meal. Here are four delectable re-interpretations of classic side dish themes. BREADS If biscuits and rolls feel too commonplace, opt for something with savory style. These Cornmeal Madeleines (opposite, top left) are flavored with buttermilk and a hint of rosemary. The recipe is on page 128. GRATINS What hides beneath a gratin's golden-brown crust? A seductive mix of butter- and cream-infused vegetables. Here (opposite, top right), the traditional potato is joined by its root sisters the turnip and the carrot. The recipe appears on page 107. VEGETABLES Some greens round out the offerings and add color to the table. The secret to these room-temperature Brussels Sprout Petals à la Grecque (opposite, bottom left) is a piquant vinaigrette. Find the recipe on page 105. STUFFINGS While every family has its favorite, if you're looking to try something new, sample individual portions of custardy Bread Pudding Stuffing with Onion Cream (opposite, bottom right). Our recipe is on page 110.

Simple Choices

With a few extra ingredients, these familiar winter staples are transformed into delectable side dishes that would grace any meal.

Brussels sprouts Toss with butter and lemon zest, chopped toasted nuts, or freshly-grated Parmesan cheese.

Carrots Toss with butter or olive oil; add chopped ginger and grated orange zest, brown sugar or maple syrup; or mix with some dried cranberries and toasted pecans.

Onions Try cipollini or pearl varieties. Halve and roast in olive oil; sprinkle with chopped thyme or sage, or balsamic or sherry vinegar.

Potatoes Roast in olive oil with sea salt and chopped rosemary, or mash with roasted garlic and fresh parsley.

Sumptuous sides are tailor-made for second helpings

With fruit The salty-sweet pairing of cheese and fruit is a very satisfying punctuation to a meal, served either French-style (after salad, before dessert) or the British and American way (following dessert). Ripe Bosc pears poached in port temper the richness of Maytag blue cheese wedges (opposite), while grilled apricots and raisin-bread rounds sweeten a mild, soft ricotta (right). The recipes are on page 129.

With cake Dried fruits such as figs, dates, cranberries or apricots are also a fine accompaniment to cheese. Rich and chewy slices of dense Date Nut Cake (left) are a perfect contrast to a creamy Italian mascarpone sprinkled with nutmeg. The only thing missing is a glass of fragrant dessert wine. The recipe is on page 122.

chapter 6

Seductive

Sweets

Breakfast Wreath
Frozen Pumpkin Souffle
Heavenly Slices
Dreamy Crèmes
Blood Orange Tartlets

After dinner, warmed by the food and engaged in lively conversation, your guests can sit back around the table or get cozy by the fire while they round off their meal with some strong coffee and a sumptuous dessert or two. For sweets-lovers, the season is rife with inspiration. Ancient spice-road treasures such as cinnamon, clove, nutmeg, and allspice fill the air with their fragrance and add warmth and depth to a wide assortment of baked goods. Nut meats, glistening apricots, plums, candied or dried fruits, and fresh citrus often find their way into desserts at this time of year. Flavors such as pumpkin, gingerbread, and cranberry are synonymous with holiday cooking. And somehow, the richness of a gooey chocolate ganache or silky pot de crème becomes a welcome after-dinner treat for even the most disciplined among us—it *is* Christmas, after all. So get out the dessert plates, pour the coffee, and let yourself succumb to all the sweet indulgence the season has to offer.

Sweet surprises Though this strudel-like pastry with almonds and apricots is known as a Breakfast Wreath (opposite), you need not wait till morning to enjoy it; recipe page 123. Traditional pumpkin pie gets a blast of winter via individual Frozen Pumpkin Souffles (above): the recipe is on page 116. Preceding pages: A drizzle of Chocolate Fudge Sauce is always a welcome embellishment (left); recipe page 114. Chocolate and hazelnut join for a memorable twist on Proust's madeleine (right); turn to page 128 for the recipe.

Heavenly slices Chocolate lovers will swoon at the very sight of this frilly Black Forest Cake (below). Underneath its seemingly prim exterior hides a decadent pairing of chocolate mousse and Chantilly cream punctuated with sour cherries. This Spiced Plum Gingerbread Cake (opposite) also holds a secret—in addition to its heady mix of ginger, cinnamon, cloves, and nutmeg, the batter is flavored with plum tea to lend a subtle sweetness. The simple confectioner's sugar icing, too, is infused with plum tea, which turns it a lovely pink. Recipes on pages 120 and 125.

baked treats

Dreamy crèmes Use the edge of your spoon to gently crack through its golden, caramelized crust, then dip into the rich, creamy center. This is no ordinary bistro dessert, but a luscious tropical version—Coconut Crème Brûlée (opposite). The ingredients of a classic Pot de Crème (right) are surprisingly simple—heavy cream, whole milk, egg yolks, and sugar— but the end result is irresistibly rich and custardy. We've flavored this one with flecks of vanilla beans, but you may want to try cocoa or coffee. These French desserts are best made in individual servings— no sharing necessary. Turn to pages 115 and 117 for the recipes.

Crème brûlée flavorings

Citrus A teaspoon or so of grated lemon, lime, orange, or even grapefruit zest will contribute a wonderfully tart edge to this creamy dessert. Whisk into the eggs before adding to the cream.

Coffee Coarsely ground espresso beans, together with a small amount of very strong coffee, gives crème brûlée a caffeinated boost. Stir these ingredients into the cream as it is heated on the burner.

Spices A ginger crème brûlée is easily made by adding a few tablespoons of very finely chopped crystallized ginger to the cream before heating. For cinnamon crème brûlée, stir 1/2 to 3/4 teaspoon ground cinnamon into the strained custard.

Liqueurs For orange crème brûlée, add about 2 tablespoons of Grand Marnier to the custard before pouring it into the ramekins. Almond-flavored amaretto will also give subtle enhancement, or add two tablespoons each of bourbon and dark rum and a pinch of nutmeg for an eggnog version.

Vanilla In this classic crème brûlée, a vanilla bean, split to expose the seeds, is added to the cream as it heats; the bean is removed, leaving the seeds behind. If vanilla beans are not available, vanilla extract is an acceptable substitute; use only pure vanilla extract, of course; add 1 1/2 teaspoons to the strained custard.

fruitful encounters

Fresh Greens Nestled into an etched-glass compote, these bite-size slices of fruit (left) glisten like precious gems. Kiwi pieces, halved green grapes, honeydew melon balls, and star fruit slices get their sheen from a coating of fragrant jasmine tea cooked in lime sugar syrup. A dollop of green-tea ice cream would continue the tea theme and match the palette of the dessert. You'll find the recipe on page 122.

Tarts of Christmas If a chocolate or custard dessert seems to be too rich of a finale to a holiday feast, think of the refreshing taste of a fruit tart. These zingy little Blood Orange Tartlets (opposite) are infused with orange juice as well as grated peel. They wear a delicate lattice of meringue and are accompanied by pâtes de fruits. Buttermilk Ice Cream is a soothing contrast to the intense flavors of a harvest-inspired Apple, Pear, and Dried Plum Tarte Tatin (right). The recipes are on pages 119 and 118.

Recipes

The recipes in this section are listed below alphabetically for easy reference. The page number for the photograph is given first; the page number for the recipe is given second, in italics.

SPICY SESAME SOY NUTS

3 tablespoons soy sauce

2 tablespoons Asian sesame oil

1 tablespoon unsalted butter

2 teaspoons honey

1 teaspoon sea salt

3 cups roasted unsalted nuts

1 1/2 tablespoons toasted sesame seeds

1/8 to 1/4 teaspoon cayenne pepper,
    or to taste

Is it possible for nuts to become even nuttier? When you coat them with sesame oil and toasted sesame seeds, the answer is a resounding yes. Pass these around as a complement to cocktails. These spicy nuts tickle the tongue with their flavorings of cayenne pepper and honey. We like to use a gourmet mix of pecans, cashews, and almonds, but the Asian-inspired seasoning will be delicious on whatever nuts you fancy.

1. Preheat the oven to 350°F. In a large bowl, combine the soy sauce, 1 tablespoon of the sesame oil, the butter, honey and salt. Add the nuts, sesame seeds and cayenne pepper and toss to coat. Spread the nuts on a baking sheet and bake, stirring once, for 15 to 20 minutes, or until golden brown and fragrant. Add the remaining 1 tablespoon sesame oil, toss to combine, and let cool. Transfer to jars or containers with lids. Stored in a cool, dark place, the nuts will keep up to 2 weeks. Makes 3 cups.

SPICY PECANS

4 tablespoons unsalted butter

3 tablespoons sugar

2 teaspoons Cajun seasoning

2 teaspoons ground cumin

1/2 teaspoon cayenne pepper

1 pound pecan halves

Need a quick fix for last-minute entertaining? These spicy pecans take just a couple of minutes to prepare. Serve a bowlful warm with a wedge of cheese and some wine when unexpected guests come to call, or pack up a boxful to give to a friend.

1. In a large skillet over medium high heat, heat the butter until it begins to foam. Add the spices and sugar and cook, stirring, until combined. Add the pecans and cook, stirring, for 3 minutes, or until toasted.

2. Transfer the pecans to a wire mesh rack set over a baking sheet and let cool to room temperature. Store in an airtight container until ready to serve. Warm before serving. Makes about 4 cups.

MINIATURE CARAMELIZED ONION TARTLETS

FOR THE PASTRY SHELLS:

1 recipe of your favorite pie dough

FOR THE CARAMELIZED ONIONS:

2 tablespoons unsalted butter

2 medium onions, preferably Vidalia, thinly sliced

1 teaspoon sugar

Salt to taste

FOR THE CUSTARD:

3 large eggs

3/4 cup heavy cream

2 tablespoons Dijon mustard

A pinch of celery salt

A pinch of cayenne pepper

The wonderful flavor and diminutive size of these French-style savory tartlets make them an excellent hors d'oeuvre for a cocktail party. Or, serve a trio of tartlets with a side salad to each guest as a light holiday lunch.

1. Make the pastry shells: Lightly spray 2 mini muffin pans with non-stick cooking spray. On a lightly floured surface, roll out the dough 1/8 inch thick. Using a 3-inch round cookie cutter, stamp out 24 circles of dough. Fill each muffin cup with a dough round, pressing it into shape. Line with paper, fill with pie weights and chill for 30 minutes.

2. Preheat the oven to 350°F. Bake the shells for 6 to 8 minutes, or until pale golden. Remove from the oven and allow to cool in the pans. When the shells are completely cool, invert the pans onto a baking sheet, then turn the shells right side up.

3. Make the onions: In a saucepan over medium heat, melt the butter. Add the onions and cook, stirring, until wilted. Reduce the heat to medium-low and cook, stirring frequently, until the onions are a rich gold. Add the sugar and salt and continue cooking until the onions are the color of brown sugar. Remove from the heat and set aside.

4. Make the custard: Whisk all the custard ingredients until well combined.

5. Preheat the oven to 350°F.

6. Assemble: Place 1/2 teaspoon caramelized onions in each pastry shell. Cover with the custard. Place the tartlets on a baking sheet. Bake for 10 to 12 minutes, or until the custard is just set. Makes 24 hors d'oeuvres.

APPLE-RUTABAGA SOUP

½ cup (1 stick) unsalted butter

1 cup coarsely chopped onion

1 cup peeled, cored, and coarsely chopped Granny Smith apple

1 cup coarsely chopped rutabaga

1 cup chopped butternut squash

1 cup coarsely chopped carrots

1 cup coarsely chopped sweet potato

Salt to taste

5 cups chicken stock

1 cup heavy cream

3 tablespoons maple syrup, or to taste

Cayenne pepper to taste

If you've ever encountered a rutabaga in the grocery store and ruminated on its possible uses, now is your chance to find out how good it can be. This large pale yellow root vegetable resembles a turnip and is actually a member of the cabbage family. Its mild flavor is the perfect partner to tart Granny Smith apples in this creamy soup. Serve the soup with the Cornmeal Madeleines on page 108 as a light lunch, or as part of a complete meal before Brine-Cured Roast Turkey (page 112), Bread Pudding Stuffing (page 110), Potato Gratin with Turnips and Carrots (page 107), and Brussels Sprout Petals à la Grecque (page 105).

1. In a large saucepan over medium-high heat, melt the butter. Add the onion, apple, rutabaga, squash, carrot, sweet potato, and ½ teaspoon salt and cook, stirring occasionally, until the onion is translucent. Add the chicken stock, bring to a boil, and simmer, stirring occasionally, for 30 to 35 minutes, or until the vegetables are tender.

2. Transfer the soup in batches to a food processor and process until smooth. Return to the saucepan, and add the cream, maple syrup, and salt and cayenne to taste. Bring to a simmer, stirring occasionally, and cook until heated through. Serves 8.

BRUSSELS SPROUT PETALS À LA GRECQUE

2 pounds brussels sprouts, rinsed

FOR THE VINAIGRETTE:

½ cup water

½ cup dry vermouth or dry white wine

1 onion, finely chopped

3 cloves garlic, minced

1 teaspoon white wine vinegar

1 teaspoon coriander seeds

½ teaspoon fennel seeds

3 tablespoons extra virgin olive oil

1 tablespoon fresh lemon juice

2 sprigs fresh thyme

½ bay leaf

½ teaspoon cracked black pepper

Salt and freshly ground pepper to taste

While you may have come to expect bright green little heads of brussels sprouts as a side dish during the winter months, here they are prepared with a twist. Not only are the sprouts served at room temperature, not warm, but the heads are separated into individual leaves, or "petals."

1. Bring a large pot of salted water to a boil. Fill a bowl with ice water.

2. Meanwhile, with a paring knife, trim the ends of the brussels sprouts and peel off the leaves one by one.

3. Add the brussels sprout petals to the boiling water and cook for about 20 seconds, or until they turn bright green. Do not overcook. Drain and refresh the petals in the ice water. Allow to chill completely, then drain and pat dry. Refrigerate until ready to serve.

4. Make the vinaigrette: In a saucepan over medium heat, combine the water, vermouth, onion, garlic and vinegar. Bring to a boil, then remove the pan from the heat and set aside.

5. Meanwhile, in a spice grinder or clean pepper mill, grind the coriander and fennel seeds. Add the olive oil, lemon juice, thyme, bay leaf, fennel, coriander, and cracked black pepper to the vermouth and vinegar mixture, stir, and cool to room temperature. Adjust the seasoning if necessary. The vinaigrette can be made up to 2 days ahead. Store covered in the refrigerator and allow to come back to room temperature before serving.

6. To serve: In a bowl, toss the brussels sprouts with the vinaigrette. Serves 8.

SPICED BEET MEDLEY

3 pounds assorted small beets—red, golden, and candy-striped (Chioggia), if available

4 tablespoons olive oil

1 teaspoon salt, or to taste

1/2 teaspoon freshly ground pepper, or to taste

1/8 to 1/4 teaspoon ground cloves, or to taste

1/8 to 1/4 teaspoon freshly grated nutmeg, or to taste

1/2 to 1 teaspoon ground coriander, or to taste

1 to 2 tablespoons sherry vinegar (available at specialty food shops)

This pretty side dish adds some color to the winter table. We recommend using a mix of different colored beets for the most impact. In addition to widely available dark purple or red beets, look for the sweet golden type and the white-and-red striped Chioggia variety.

1. Preheat the oven to 400°F.

2. Trim the stems of the beets to 1 inch and scrub well. Arrange them in a shallow baking pan large enough to hold them in one layer. Add 2 tablespoons of the olive oil and turn to coat. Bake for 45 minutes to 1 hour, or until the beets can be pierced easily with a knife.

3. Cool the beets until they can be handled, and remove the skins. Cut the beets into bite-sized pieces, keeping colors separate until serving time so that the darker beets will not discolor the lighter ones.

4. In a bowl, combine the remaining 2 tablespoons olive oil with the salt, pepper, spices, and vinegar. Drizzle over beets (in separate bowls) and toss gently. The beets can be prepared up to this point 1 day ahead; chill, covered.

5. To serve: If the beets have been chilled, let sit at room temperature for an hour. Transfer to a serving dish. Serves 6.

POTATO GRATIN WITH TURNIPS AND CARROTS

4 tablespoons unsalted butter

1 onion, thinly sliced

1 quart heavy cream

2 cups milk

2 tablespoons kosher salt, or to taste

1 teaspoon white pepper

Freshly grated nutmeg to taste

4 medium to large turnips, peeled and
sliced ¼ inch thick

4 medium to large potatoes,
peeled and sliced ¼ inch thick

6 medium-large carrots,
sliced ¼ inch thick

The addition of turnips and carrots lends a sumptuous sweetness to a classic French potato gratin. Warm and rich, it is a comforting treat on a cold winter's eve. Serve the gratin with the Bread Pudding Stuffing on page 110 and the Brussels Sprout Petals à la Grecque on page 105 as a series of side dishes for the Brine-Cured Roast Turkey on page 112.

1. Preheat the oven to 375°F. Butter a large shallow baking dish.

2. In a large casserole over medium heat, melt half the butter. Add the onion and cook, stirring occasionally, for 5 minutes, or until translucent. Add the cream and milk, bring to a boil, and season with the salt, pepper, and nutmeg. Add the turnips, potatoes, and carrots, folding them in with a spatula until completely coated. Simmer the vegetables until the cream begins to thicken and the vegetables are almost tender, about 8 minutes. They should not be completely cooked.

3. Transfer the vegetable mixture to the buttered baking dish and dot the top of the vegetables with the remaining butter. The dish can be assembled 1 day ahead; store in the refrigerator, covered.

4. Bake in the upper third of the oven for 15 to 20 minutes, or until the top is golden brown and the vegetables are tender. Serves 8 to 10.

CORNMEAL MADELEINES

6 tablespoons unsalted butter, softened

1/2 cup sugar

1 large egg, lightly beaten

1 1/4 cups all-purpose flour

1 cup plus 2 tablespoons cornmeal

1/2 teaspoon baking powder

1/8 teaspoon baking soda

1/2 teaspoon salt

1/2 tablespoon finely chopped garlic

1 tablespoon finely chopped fresh
  rosemary

1 cup buttermilk

Fragrant with rosemary and garlic, shell-shaped cornmeal madeleines are a step above their common muffin cousins. Serve them as a side dish as part of a dinner featuring the Apple-Rutabaga Soup and Brine-Cured Roast Turkey on pages 104 and 112, or pair them with your own warming chowders, chilis, or stews.

1. Preheat the oven to 350°F. Spray two madeleine tins with nonstick vegetable spray.

2. In a medium bowl with an electric mixer, cream together the butter and sugar until light and fluffy. Add the egg and beat just until combined.

3. In another bowl, combine the flour, cornmeal, baking powder, baking soda, salt, garlic, and rosemary. With the mixer on low, alternately add the dry ingredients and buttermilk to the butter mixture, scraping the sides and bottom of the bowl occasionally.

4. Fill the madeleine molds halfway with batter. Bake for 5 to 7 minutes, or until golden. Let cool for 5 minutes and invert onto racks. Continue baking madeleines in the same manner with the remaining batter. Makes about 48 madeleines.

WILD RICE PILAF

3 tablespoons unsalted butter

2 leeks, white parts only, thinly sliced
and washed

2 carrots, finely chopped

1 celery stalk, finely chopped

1/2 cup dry sherry

1 1/2 cups wild rice

1 1/2 teaspoons salt, or to taste

1/2 teaspoon freshly ground pepper,
or to taste

1 cinnamon stick

3 cups vegetable or chicken stock or
canned broth

1/2 cup diced dried apricots

1/2 cup slivered or chopped lightly
toasted pistachios

Enhanced with the flavor of dried apricots and pistachios, this rice is a savory substitute for stuffing. When accompanying a Crown Roast of Lamb (see page 113), you don't even need a serving bowl. Simply spoon the rice into the enter of the roast before bringing it to the table—use any extra rice to garnish the platter along with sprigs of fresh herbs.

1. In a large saucepan over medium heat, melt the butter. Add the vegetables and cook, stirring occasionally, for 5 minutes. Do not brown. Add the sherry and simmer for 5 minutes.

2. Stir in the rice, salt, pepper, and cinnamon. Add the stock and bring to a boil, then reduce to a simmer. Simmer, covered, for 40 to 50 minutes, or until the rice is tender and most of the liquid is absorbed. Remove from the heat and stir in the apricots and pistachios. Remove the cinnamon stick and adjust the seasoning if necessary. Serves 6.

BREAD PUDDING STUFFING WITH ONION CREAM

FOR THE STUFFING:

2 cups (bulk) pork sausage

6 tablespoons ($^3/_4$ stick) unsalted butter

1 large onion, finely chopped

1 celery stalk, finely chopped and 2 tablespoons minced celery leaves

1 Granny Smith apple, peeled, cored, and finely chopped

$^1/_2$ cup chopped pecans

2 cups stale corn bread crumbled into $^1/_4$-inch pieces

4 cups stale white bread crumbled into $^1/_4$-inch pieces

1 large egg, lightly beaten

$^1/_4$ cup applesauce

$^1/_2$ cup turkey or chicken stock

1 tablespoon minced fresh sage

1 tablespoon minced fresh thyme

Salt and freshly ground pepper to taste

FOR THE CUSTARD:

4 large eggs

2 cups heavy cream

FOR THE ONION CREAM:

6 tablespoons unsalted butter

4 cups finely chopped onions

$^1/_4$ cup all-purpose flour

2 cups milk

$^1/_2$ cup heavy cream

Salt and white pepper to taste

Freshly grated nutmeg to taste

Topped with a savory onion-cream sauce, these cute and custardy pint-sized puddings are an elegant way to serve stuffing.

1. Make the stuffing: Preheat the oven to 350°F. In a large skillet over medium-high heat, sauté the sausage until cooked through. Drain and set aside.

2. In a large saucepan over medium heat, melt the butter. Add the onion and celery and cook, stirring, until the onion becomes translucent. Add the apple, pecans, and sausage. Cook, stirring, for 2 minutes more. Remove from the heat. Mix in the corn bread and white bread until well combined. Add the egg, applesauce, stock, minced herbs, celery leaves, and salt and pepper.

3. Transfer the stuffing to a 9- by 12-inch baking pan and cover with foil. Bake for 20 minutes. Let cool to room temperature, then crumble into small pieces and reserve. The stuffing can be prepared up to 2 days in advance; keep covered and chilled.

4. Preheat the oven to 350°F. Grease twenty-four 3-ounce ramekins with butter.

5. Make the custard: In a bowl, combine the eggs and the cream. Fill each mold $^3/_4$ full with stuffing; do not pack tightly. Pour the custard mixture on top of the stuffing to just below the lip of each ramekin. Set the molds in a large shallow baking pan. Pour enough hot water into the pan to reach 1$^1/_2$ inches up the sides of the molds and bake for 25 minutes, or until the custard is just set.

6. While the stuffing bakes, make the onion cream: In a 4-quart saucepan over medium heat, melt the butter. Add the onions and cook, stirring occasionally, until translucent. Add the flour and cook, stirring, for 5 minutes.

7. Meanwhile, in another saucepan, scald the milk and cream together. Whisk the hot cream mixture into the onions until thoroughly combined. Simmer over low heat, stirring occasionally, for 10 minutes. The sauce should be thick enough to coat the back of a spoon. Season with salt, pepper, and nutmeg. Strain the sauce through a sieve, if desired. Keep warm until ready to serve.

8. Carefully remove the pan of ramekins from the oven and take the molds out of the water bath. Unmold by running the point of a paring knife around the edge of each ramekin, then invert and place onto a platter. Top with the onion cream sauce. Pass the remaining sauce in a gravy boat. Serves 8.

PASTA IN CHAMPAGNE SAUCE WITH GOLDEN CAVIAR

1 shallot, minced

1 cup Champagne

1/2 to 1 cup crème fraîche, to taste

Salt to taste

1/4 teaspoon white pepper,
   or to taste

1 pound fresh angel hair pasta

2 ounces golden caviar (American
   whitefish caviar)

2 tablespoons minced fresh tarragon

This delicate pasta has a surprising twist—glistening golden caviar sprinkled throughout like colorful confetti. The golden variety has an American provenance and is milder (and much less expensive) than its fancy overseas cousins. While this dish is delicious as a light meal, because it is so festive we like to serve it as an appetizer for our New Year's Eve menu centered around a Crown Roast of Lamb (see page 113).

1. Bring a large pot of salted water to a boil.

2. In a large skillet over medium high heat, combine the shallot and Champagne and simmer until the mixture is reduced by half. Add the crème fraîche and simmer until lightly thickened. Remove from the heat and season with the salt and pepper.

3. Add the pasta to the boiling water and cook, stirring occasionally, for 3 minutes, or until al dente. Drain the pasta and transfer it to the skillet. Gently toss over medium-low heat until heated through. Stir in half the caviar.

4. Divide the pasta among six salad plates and garnish each with a portion of the remaining caviar and a sprinkling of tarragon. Serves 6.

BRINE-CURED ROAST TURKEY

FOR THE BRINE:

3¼ cups sugar

1¼ cups kosher salt

2 cups honey

6 sprigs each fresh parsley, dill, thyme, tarragon, and sage

2 sprigs fresh rosemary

2 tablespoons mustard seeds

2 tablespoons fennel seeds

2 cinnamon sticks

5 bay leaves

8 whole cloves

1 tablespoon juniper berries

2 tablespoons whole black peppercorns

2 lemons, cut in half

1 tablespoon whole allspice berries

2 gallons boiling water

One 18- to 20-pound fresh turkey

1 pound unsalted butter, melted

"Curing" a turkey overnight in an herb-infused brine results in meat that is both flavorful and extremely moist. Be sure to use only a fresh turkey for this technique, however—frozen, self-basing, and kosher turkeys have already been salted, and the brine would make them too salty. You will need a container large enough to hold the turkey in the brine (and ample refrigerator space for the setup); if you don't have a large stockpot (or lobster pot), simply buy an inexpensive plastic wastebasket large enough to hold the bird. Otherwise, the procedure is simplicity itself, and the results wonderfully satisfying. If you like, decorate the serving platter with sprigs of rosemary to echo the woodsy flavor of the brine.

1. Combine the brine ingredients in a large container, pouring the boiling water in last. Stir to dissolve the sugar and salt, then let cool to room temperature. Add the turkey, cover, and refrigerate overnight.

2. Preheat the oven to 300°F.

3. Remove the turkey from the brine and rinse under cold water. Cover the entire turkey with cheesecloth and place in a large roasting pan. Using a brush, saturate the cloth with some of the melted butter. Roast for 3 to 4 hours, basting the cheesecloth with the butter every 30 minutes. The turkey is done when the thigh-joint temperature reaches 175-180°F.

4. Remove the turkey from the oven and let it rest for 30 minutes.

5. Carefully remove the cheesecloth and transfer the turkey to a platter. Serves 8 to 10.

CROWN ROAST OF LAMB

1 crown roast of lamb, consisting of 2
    racks of lamb (14 to 16 chops),
    bones frenched

2 teaspoons coarse salt, or to taste

1 teaspoon freshly ground pepper

1 large navel orange, scrubbed

2 small heads garlic, cut in half
    parallel to the root end

1 large bunch fresh thyme

1 recipe Wild Rice Pilaf (see page 109)

Named for its shape, this roast is fit for a king (or, more likely, a special dinner for New Year's Eve). Ask your butcher to french the roast for you, trimming the little chop "handles" of all fat; you can even decorate their ends with paper frills, if you like. Once the roast has cooked, it can rest while a course of Pasta in Champagne Sauce with Golden Caviar (see page 111) is served.

1. Preheat the oven to 500°F. Place roast in a roasting pan and season with the salt and pepper. Stuff the orange into the center of the roast, to flavor it and help hold its shape. Place the garlic, cut side down, on top of the orange. Arrange the thyme sprigs between the chops and on top of the roast; reserve a few sprigs for garnish.

2. Roast for 10 minutes. Reduce the temperature to 350°F and continue to roast for 30 to 35 minutes more, or until the chops have reached an internal temperature of 125° to 130°F for medium-rare. Remove from the oven and let rest for 15 minutes.

3. Place the roast on a platter. Remove and discard the orange, garlic, and thyme. Spoon the pilaf into center of roast and garnish with the reserved thyme sprigs. Serves 4 to 6.

BUTTERMILK ICE CREAM

5 large egg yolks

1½ cups sugar

2 cups milk

2 cups heavy cream

½ vanilla bean, split lengthwise

1¼ cups buttermilk

While it may look like play-by-the-rules vanilla, this ice cream will surprise your guests with its piquant buttermilk flavor. Serve a scoop alongside a generous slice of the hearty Apple, Pear, and Dried Plum Tart Tatin on page 118 for a delicious dessert.

1. In the top of a double boiler placed over simmering water, whisk together the egg yolks and sugar until the mixture becomes slightly thickened and foamy.
2. Meanwhile, in a saucepan, combine the milk, cream, and vanilla bean and scald.
3. Slowly pour the hot milk mixture into the egg mixture, whisking constantly, and continue to cook over medium heat until the custard coats the back of a spoon. Remove from the heat, strain, and cool to room temperature.
4. Add the buttermilk. Freeze in an ice-cream maker according to the manufacturer's instructions. Makes about 1 quart.

CHOCOLATE FUDGE SAUCE

1 cup heavy cream

6 ounces unsweetened chocolate, coarsely chopped

2/3 cup sugar

1/3 cup light corn syrup

3 tablespoons unsalted butter

1½ teaspoons vanilla extract

A pinch of salt

Spoon this rich classic fudge sauce over an after-dinner piece of cake or scoop of sorbet—try a tart raspberry sorbet, the colors mix beautifully—for dinner-party guests or to top a yummy sundae as a midnight snack after an evening of wrapping presents. Any leftovers will keep for weeks.

1. In a saucepan, bring the cream to a simmer. Stir in the chocolate, sugar, corn syrup and butter. Simmer, stirring frequently, until the chocolate melts. Cook at a low boil for 5 minutes, stirring occasionally. Remove from the heat. Stir in the vanilla and salt. Transfer to a bowl and cool to room temperature.
2. When the sauce is cool, transfer to jars with tightly fitting lids. Store in the refrigerator for up to 1 month. Makes about 2½ cups.

COCONUT CRÈME BRÛLÉE

1 quart heavy cream

1 cup dried unsweetened (desiccated) coconut (available at specialty food stores or Indian markets)

$\frac{1}{2}$ cup vanilla sugar (or substitute 1 teaspoon vanilla extract and $\frac{1}{2}$ cup granulated sugar)

9 large egg yolks

$\frac{1}{2}$ cup granulated sugar for the crust

While crème brûlée is decidedly French, this one has a tropical flair thanks to the flaky coconut hidden under its crispy crust. The secret to a luscious crene brulee is to use wide shallow molds—no more than 1 inch high—so the custard cooks evenly in the water bath and is a creamy and delicate contrast to the carmelized sugar topping. Broil about two inches from the heat with the door open so the custard doesn't cook further.

1. Preheat the oven to 300°F. Have ready 8 round crème brûlée molds, 1 inch deep by 4 inches in diameter.

2. In a saucepan over medium heat, combine the cream, coconut, and vanilla sugar (if using regular sugar, add the vanilla extract to the strained custard), bring to a boil and simmer over medium-low heat, stirring occasionally, for 30 minutes.

3. Meanwhile, in a large bowl, whisk the egg yolks. Strain the cream mixture into a large measuring cup and pour it in a stream, whisking, into the egg yolks. Strain again into the measuring cup and carefully skim the foam from the surface. Pour the custard into the molds and transfer them to a large baking pan. Add water to the baking pan to reach halfway up the sides of the molds. Bake for 1 hour or until just set. Remove molds and cool to room temperature.

4. Preheat the broiler. Sprinkle a thin layer of sugar on each crème brûlée. Place under the broiler until a golden-brown crust covers the surface, carefully turning the molds as necessary for even carmelizing. Serve immediately. Serves 8.

FROZEN PUMPKIN SOUFFLÉS

1 cup granulated sugar

1/2 cup water

6 large egg whites

1 quart heavy cream

2/3 cup confectioners' sugar

1 1/2 cups solid pack pumpkin

1 1/2 teaspoons ground cinnamon

1 teaspoon freshly grated nutmeg

1/4 teaspoon ground cloves

1/4 teaspoon ground allspice

1 tablespoon vanilla extract or the
    seeds from 1 vanilla bean

2 cups finely chopped toasted pecans

1/2 cup toasted pumpkin seeds

These individual soufflés will win over even the staunchest traditionalist at your holiday feast. All the flavors of the familiar pumpkin pie are here—cinnamon, nutmeg, cloves, and allspice— in a cool, creamy frozen custard. A garnish of toasted pecan and pumpkin seeds adds a crunchy counterpoint to the smooth cream. And, although these mimic the appearance of the classic hot soufflé, rising high above the tops of their ramekins, there is no need to worry about last-minute preparation—they can be made up to a day ahead (and they're guaranteed not to fall!)

1. Prepare the molds: You will need eight 6-ounce ramekins or soufflé molds. Cut two 14-inch-long sheets of parchment paper or waxed paper lengthwise into 2-inch strips. Wrap a strip around the outside of a ramekin to make a collar extending 1 1/2 inches above the top edge of the dish and secure with tape. Repeat with the remaining ramekins.

2. In a small saucepan over medium heat, combine the granulated sugar with the 1/2 cup water. Bring to a boil, stirring to dissolve the sugar, then cook, without stirring, until the sugar syrup registers 240°F to 246°F on a candy thermometer. Remove from the heat.

3. Meanwhile, in a large bowl with an electric mixer, beat the egg whites to soft peaks. Beating constantly, slowly pour the hot sugar into the egg whites in a thin stream. Once all of the sugar has been added, whip the egg white mixture on high speed until it is cool and forms stiff peaks.

4. Meanwhile, in a bowl, combine 3 1/2 cups of the heavy cream with the confectioners' sugar and beat until the mixture forms soft peaks.

5. In a large bowl, whisk together the pumpkin, the remaining 1/2 cup cream, cinnamon, nutmeg, cloves, allspice, and vanilla. Fold the egg whites into the pumpkin mixture. Then fold in the whipped cream until no trace of white shows.

6. Divide the pumpkin mixture among the ramekins, filling them almost to the top of the paper collars. Freeze for at least 6 hours, or overnight.

7. Remove the parchment-paper collars and roll the sides of the soufflés in the toasted pecans. Allow to sit at room temperature for about 5 minutes before serving. Garnish each with a few toasted pumpkin seeds. Serves 8.

POTS DE CRÈME

1 cup heavy cream

²/₃ cup milk

2 vanilla beans, split lengthwise

4 large egg yolks

¹/₃ cup sugar

It's hard to believe how just a few simple ingredients—cream, milk, eggs, sugar, and vanilla—can result in such a luxurious and velvety dessert. In lieu of standard ramekins, a selection of mismatched vintage custard cups would be a pretty way to serve these pots de crème.

1. In a saucepan set over medium heat combine the cream, milk, and vanilla beans and bring just to a simmer. Remove from the heat and let infuse for 30 minutes. Then remove the vanilla beans; scrape the seeds into the cream mixture.

2. In a large bowl, with an electric mixer, beat the yolks with the sugar until the mixture is pale yellow and falls back into the bowl in a ribbon when the beaters are lifted. Whisk in the cream mixture and strain the mixture into a bowl. Let stand for 15 minutes, then skim the surface of all foam.

3. Preheat oven to 325°F.

4. Divide the custard among four 4-ounce ramekins. Place them in a shallow baking pan and add enough hot water to reach halfway up the sides of the ramekins. Bake, covered loosely with buttered foil, for 20 to 25 minutes, or until the sides are set but the centers remain jiggly. Let cool to room temperature and chill before serving. Serves 4.

APPLE, PEAR AND DRIED PLUM TARTE TATIN

FOR THE PASTRY:

1½ cups all-purpose flour

¼ teaspoon salt

½ cup (1 stick) cold unsalted butter,
   cut into bits

¼ cup ice water

FOR THE FILLING:

½ cup (1 stick) unsalted
   butter, softened

½ cup sugar

1 pound apples, peeled, cored,
   and quartered

1 pound pears, such as D'Anjou,
   peeled, quartered and cored

½ pound dried plums (prunes)

This upside-down French apple tart is named after the Tatin sisters who allegedly invented it at their Loire Valley restaurant at the turn of the nineteenth century. The modern-day addition of pears and dried plums gives the tart a rustic flavor. Serve hearty wedges with a dollop of the Buttermilk Ice Cream on page 114 as a wonderful finish to a festive dinner.

1. Make the pastry: In a food processor, combine the flour and salt and pulse to combine. Add the cold butter and pulse until the mixture resembles coarse meal. Add the ice water and process just until dough begins to come together. Form the dough into a disk, wrap in plastic, and chill for 1 hour.

2. Preheat the oven to 375°F.

3. Melt 3 tablespoons of the butter. Set aside.

4. Generously coat a tarte Tatin pan or a 10-inch ovenproof nonstick skillet with the remaining 5 tablespoons butter. Sprinkle with ¼ cup of the sugar. Arrange the fruit in a tight circular pattern. Drizzle with reserved melted butter. Sprinkle with the remaining ¼ cup sugar.

5. Place the pan over medium heat and cook until the sugar begins to turn a deep, rich brown. Remove from the heat.

6. Meanwhile, on a floured board, roll the chilled dough out to a thickness of 1⅛ inch. Trim the dough into a circle 10 inches in diameter.

7. Place the circle of dough on top of the caramelized fruit. Bake the tart for about 35 minutes, or until the crust is golden brown on the lower third of the oven. Remove from the oven and let the tart cool slightly.

8. Place a 12-inch serving plate upside down on top of the pan. Using pot holders, invert the tart onto the plate. Carefully lift off the pan. Serve warm, with buttermilk ice cream. Serves 8.

BLOOD ORANGE TARTLETS

FOR THE PASTRY:

1/2 cup toasted hazelnuts

1 1/2 cups all-purpose flour

2 tablespoons confectioners' sugar

1/2 teaspoon salt

6 tablespoons cold unsalted butter, cut into bits

About 1/4 cup ice water

FOR THE FILLING:

2/3 cup fresh blood orange juice or regular orange juice

2 tablespoons fresh lemon juice

1/2 cup sugar

1 tablespoon grated blood orange zest or regular orange zest

4 large eggs

FOR THE MERINGUE:

3 large egg whites

A pinch of salt

1/4 teaspoon cream of tartar

1/2 teaspoon vanilla extract

1/4 cup superfine sugar

Blood oranges have bright red or red-streaked flesh, and their sweet-tart juice adds a gorgeous red hue to these tartlets. Once only available imported from the Mediterranean, blood oranges are now grown in California and can be found in specialty markets and even some supermarkets from late fall through the spring. If you can't find them, however, just substitute regular orange juice and zest.

1. Make the pastry: In a food processor, process the nuts until finely ground. Add the flour, sugar, and salt. Pulse to mix. Add the butter and pulse until the mixture resembles coarse meal. Add 3 tablespoons of the water and pulse until the dough just comes together, adding a little additional water if necessary. Transfer the dough to a work surface. Gently knead into a ball, then flatten into a disk. Chill, wrapped in plastic, for 1 hour.

2. Preheat the oven to 375°F. Divide the dough into 6 pieces. Fit each one into a 5-inch tartlet mold with a removable bottom. Trim the edges and lightly prick the bottom of each with a fork. Transfer to freezer for 15 minutes.

3. Place the tart pans on a baking sheet and bake for 15 minutes, or until the edges are lightly browned. Let cool. Reduce oven temperature to 350°F.

4. Make the filling: In a medium bowl, whisk together the orange juice, lemon juice, and sugar. Add the grated zest and eggs and whisk to combine. Divide the filling among the tartlet shells. Bake for 15 minutes, or until the filling is set. Remove from the oven and let cool.

5. Make the meringue: In a large bowl with an electric mixer, beat the whites on low speed until foamy. Add the salt, the cream of tartar, and vanilla; increase the speed to medium-high and beat until the whites form soft peaks. Add the sugar 1 tablespoon at a time, beating until whites are stiff and glossy. Transfer the meringue to a pastry bag fitted with a medium star tip. Pipe a decorative pattern onto each tartlet. Lightly brown the meringue using a small kitchen torch, or place under a preheated broiler until golden. These are best on the day they are made, but they can be made early in the day and refrigerated. Makes 6 tartlets.

BLACK FOREST CAKE

FOR THE CAKE:

6 large eggs, separated, at room
 temperature

1 cup sugar

1½ teaspoons vanilla extract

¼ teaspoon salt

¼ teaspoon cream of tartar

⅔ cup cake flour

⅓ cup Dutch-process cocoa

FOR THE MOUSSE:

8 ounces bittersweet chocolate, chopped

6 tablespoons unsalted butter, softened

4 large egg yolks

2 tablespoons orange-flavored liqueur,
 or to taste

1 teaspoon grated orange zest

¼ cup sugar

½ teaspoon vanilla extract

1 cup heavy cream

FOR THE SUGAR SYRUP:

⅓ cup water

⅓ cup sugar

⅓ cup dark rum

The signs of a true Black Forest Cake are rich, chocolatey cake alternating with layers of kirsch-soaked cherries and Chantilly cream. This sophisticated version features a chocolate ganache coating; if you are experienced in working with chocolate, you can create a frilly ruffle to decorate its top. This decadent cake is a fabulous finishing touch for a holiday meal; if you bring it as a hostess gift for a dinner-party treat, you just may steal the show.

1. Make the cake: Preheat the oven to 350°F. Butter a 10-by-2-inch round cake pan or a 9-inch springform pan and lightly flour it, shaking out the excess.

2. In a bowl, with an electric mixer, beat the yolks until combined. Add ¾ cup of the sugar a little at a time, and beat until the mixture falls in a thick ribbon when the beaters are lifted. Beat in the vanilla.

3. In another bowl, with clean beaters, beat the whites with the salt until frothy. Add the cream of tartar and beat until the whites form very soft peaks. Beat in the remaining ¼ cup sugar a little at a time and beat the whites until they hold firm peaks. Fold the whites gently but thoroughly into the batter.

4. Sift the flour with the cocoa onto a sheet of waxed paper. Fold the flour into the egg mixture in batches, until just combined. Pour the batter into the pan and bake in the middle of the oven for 25 to 30 minutes, or until a cake tester inserted into the center comes out clean. Let the cake cool in the pan for 5 minutes. Then invert onto a rack (remove the sides of a springform pan, if using, invert, and lift off the pan bottom), peel off the waxed paper, and let cool completely.

5. Make the mousse: In the top of a double boiler set over simmering water, melt the chocolate, stirring frequently. Add the butter and stir until smooth. Remove from the water. In a heatproof bowl, with an electric mixer, beat the egg yolks, liqueur, orange zest, sugar, and vanilla to blend. Put the bowl over the simmering water and continue to beat until the mixture thickens. Remove from the heat and beat the mixture until cool. Beat in the chocolate mixture. In another bowl, beat the cream until it holds soft peaks. Fold the cream into the chocolate mixture. Chill, covered, until ready to use.

FOR THE CHERRY FILLING:

1 pound pitted sour cherries, drained if canned or frozen (reserve 3 tablespoons of the liquid if you are not using the kirsch)

1/4 to 1/3 cup sugar, or to taste

1/2 teaspoon ground cinnamon

2 tablespoons kirsch (optional)

1 tablespoon cornstarch

FOR THE CHANTILLY CREAM

1 cup heavy cream

2 to 3 tablespoons confectioners' sugar, or to taste

1/2 teaspoon vanilla extract

FOR THE CHOCOLATE GANACHE COATING:

1 cup heavy cream

8 ounces bittersweet chocolate, chopped

FOR THE GARNISH:

Chocolate ruffle (optional)*

Edible or candied flowers (optional)

6. Make the sugar syrup: In a saucepan, combine the sugar and water and heat, stirring until the sugar is dissolved. Off the heat, stir in the rum. Let cool.

7. Make the cherry filling: In a saucepan, combine the cherries, sugar, and cinnamon. Bring to a boil and simmer, stirring occasionally, for 5 minutes. Meanwhile, combine the kirsch (or reserved cherry liquid) with the cornstarch. Stir into the cherry mixture and simmer, stirring, until thickened. Transfer to a bowl, let cool, and chill, covered, until ready to use.

8. Make the Chantilly cream: In a chilled bowl, combine the cream, sugar, and vanilla and beat with chilled beaters until the cream forms soft peaks.

9. Assemble the cake: Slice the cake into 3 layers. Transfer the bottom layer, cut side up, to a cardboard round. Brush the cut side of the bottom layer with a third of the sugar syrup and spread with half the mousse filling. Spoon half the cherries over the mousse and top with a layer of half the Chantilly cream. Repeat with the second layer. Top with the last layer and moisten with the remaining syrup. Chill the cake until the mousse sets.

10. Make the ganache coating: In a saucepan over medium heat, bring the cream to a boil. Remove the pan from the heat, add the chocolate, and let stand for 2 minutes. Whisk the chocolate until smooth and strain it into a bowl. Let cool to room temperature.

11. Place the cake on a rack set in a jelly-roll or roasting pan. Pour the glaze over the cake, beginning in the center and allowing it to spread down the sides. Let stand until completely cool.

12. For the optional garnish: Decorate the top with a chocolate ruffle or edible or candied flowers. Makes one 10-inch cake.

* To purchase chocolate ruffles, contact Albert Uster Imports: (800) 231-8154.

FRUITS IN JASMINE TEA SYRUP

¹/₃ cup water

2 teaspoons jasmine tea leaves

¹/₂ cup sugar

Grated zest of 1 lime

Juice of 1 lime

3 kiwis, peeled and sliced

1 ripe honeydew melon (about 5
    pounds), halved, seeded, and flesh
    scooped into little balls or diced

8 ounces seedless green grapes,
    stemmed, washed, and cut in half

2 to 3 star fruits, sliced

Sprigs of fresh mint for garnish

This recipe couldn't be simpler, yet its jasmine fragrance and exquisite color give it a great deal of sophistication. With their fresh flavors and jewel-like hues, the fruits would be a welcome greeting as part of breakfast on Christmas morning or New Year's Day. Serve in individual glass compotes to show off the fruits' colors.

1. Bring the water just to a boil in a small saucepan. Add the jasmine tea, remove the pan from the heat, and let infuse for 4 to 5 minutes.

2. Strain the tea into a clean pan, pressing to extract as much liquid as possible; discard the leaves. Add the sugar and lime zest, place over medium heat, and stir until the sugar dissolves, then bring to a boil. Reduce the heat and simmer the syrup for 1 to 2 minutes. Remove the pan from the heat and stir in the lime juice.

3. Place the kiwi, melon, grapes, and star fruit in a serving bowl and pour on the syrup. Cover and macerate in the refrigerator for 4 to 6 hours.

4. Remove the fruit from the refrigerator at least 20 minutes before serving. Toss gently, and garnish with mint. Serves 6

Recipe from Eat Tea *(The Lyons Press), by Joanna Pruess and John Harney.*

SWEETENED SPICED MASCARPONE

8 ounces mascarpone cheese,
    softened

¹/₄ cup confectioners' sugar

¹/₂ teaspoon ground cinnamon

Mascarpone is a rich, creamy Italian cheese, often used in desserts such as tiramisu. In this recipe from food stylist Roscoe Betsill, it is flavored with cinnamon and served with a sweet fruit cake; tea cake or lemon or chocolate pound cake would also make a good partner.

1. In a medium bowl, with a wooden spoon, combine the softened cheese, sugar, and cinnamon.

2. Serve at room temperature with dates and toasted almonds or as pictured with a Spanish date and almond cake.* Add a little lavender honey to complete each serving.

*Available at Garden of Eden, New York, 212-675-6300

BREAKFAST WREATH

FOR THE DOUGH:

Two ¼-ounce packages active dry yeast

½ cup warm water

½ cup milk, heated to lukewarm

⅓ cup plus 1 teaspoon sugar

½ cup (1 stick) unsalted
   butter, softened

1 large egg, lightly beaten

1 tablespoon grated orange zest

½ teaspoon salt

½ teaspoon ground cinnamon

3 to 3½ cups all-purpose flour

FOR THE FILLING:

½ cup chopped toasted almonds

½ cup finely diced candied apricots

⅓ cup firmly packed light brown sugar

2 tablespoons unsalted butter, melted

1½ teaspoons grated orange zest

½ teaspoon ground cinnamon

A pinch of salt

2 tablespoons unsalted butter, melted

1 large egg, beaten with 1 teaspoon
   water, for egg glaze

FOR THE ICING:

1 cup confectioners' sugar

2 to 3 tablespoons milk or cream

Sliced almonds, for garnish

Here is a delicious—and thoughtful—gift to give to a friend you know will be entertaining on Christmas morning, or a festive treat you can make for your own guests. Bake the night before and store wrapped in plastic, then reheat or toast slices before serving to bring out the flavor of the candied apricots, and pair with strong-brewed coffee.

1. Make the dough: Combine the yeast, water, milk, and 1 teaspoon of the sugar in a bowl. Let proof for 5 minutes, or until bubbly.

2. In a bowl, with an electric mixer, combine the remaining ⅓ cup sugar with the butter and beat on medium until light and fluffy. Beat in the egg a little at a time, the orange zest, salt, and cinnamon. Beat in the yeast mixture and 1 cup of the flour until combined. Stir in the remaining 2 cups flour until a soft, slightly sticky dough is formed, adding up to ½ cup more flour, if necessary. Turn the dough out onto a lightly floured surface and knead until smooth and elastic, 6 to 7 minutes. Transfer the dough to a buttered bowl, turn it to coat with butter, and cover with plastic and a dish towel. Let rise in a warm place for 1½ hours, or until doubled in bulk.

3. Meanwhile, make the filling: In a bowl, combine all the ingredients.

4. Line a baking sheet with parchment paper or butter it.

5. Punch down the dough. On a lightly floured surface, roll it into a 12- by 18-inch rectangle. Brush the dough with the melted butter and spread the filling over the dough to within 1 inch of the edges.

6. Starting at a long side, roll up the dough jelly-roll fashion. Transfer to the baking sheet, form into a ring and pinch the ends together to seal. With kitchen shears, cut the dough at 1½-inch intervals, being careful to cut only up to ½ inch of the inner edge. Carefully turn each cut section to lie flat on the baking sheet so that the filling is showing. Cover loosely with plastic and let rise for 1 hour.

7. Preheat the oven to 350°F. Brush the dough with the egg glaze. Bake for 15 to 20 minutes, or until golden brown; cover loosely with foil if it begins to overbrown. Cool for 10 minutes on the baking sheet. Transfer to a rack to cool completely.

8. Make the icing: In a bowl, whisk the ingredients until smooth. Drizzle the wreath with the icing, garnish with sliced almonds. Makes one wreath.

BÛCHE DE NOËL

FOR THE CAKE:

1 1/2 cups cake flour

1 teaspoon baking soda

1/2 teaspoon salt

2/3 cup unsweetened cocoa powder,
    preferably Dutch-process

2/3 cup boiling water

3/4 cup (1 1/2 sticks) unsalted butter,
    softened

1 cup granulated sugar

1 cup firmly packed light brown sugar

2 large eggs, beaten lightly

2 teaspoons vanilla extract

1/2 cup sour cream

FOR THE FROSTING:

1 cup heavy cream

1/2 cup (1 stick) unsalted butter, cut
    into tablespoons

1/3 cup light corn syrup

1/3 cup unsweetened cocoa, preferably
    Dutch-process

A pinch of salt

12 ounces bittersweet chocolate, finely
    chopped

1 1/2 teaspoons vanilla extract

Chocolate shavings and confectioners'
    sugar, for decoration

The classic French "Yule log," a traditional Christmas cake, is re-invented here as an easy-to-assemble layer cake rather than a filled sponge roll—even a baking novice can make it. Feeling creative? Finely crush some pistachios and sprinkle over the cupcake "knots" to create "moss," or craft some "mushrooms" from meringue or marzipan to dot the log in true forest fashion.

1. Make the cake: Preheat the oven to 350°F. Butter two 7-inch springform pans. Line with waxed paper and butter and flour the paper, shaking out the excess. Butter two individual muffin cups well.

2. In a bowl, combine the cocoa with the boiling water. Whisk until smooth. Let cool. In another bowl, whisk together cake flour, baking soda, and salt.

3. In a bowl with an electric mixer, cream the butter. Add the sugars a little at a time. Beat until fluffy. Add the eggs a little at a time and the vanilla. Beat in the cocoa mixture just until combined well. Beat in the flour mixture alternately with the sour cream, ending with the flour.

4. Fill the two muffin cups 2/3 full with the batter. Divide the rest of the batter between the two cake pans. Place the cake pans and muffin pan in the oven. Bake the muffins for 15 to 18 minutes, or until a cake tester inserted in the center comes out clean. Let the muffins cool in the pan for 5 minutes, then invert onto racks to cool completely. Bake the cake layers for 35 to 40 minutes, or until a cake tester inserted in the center comes out clean. Let cool in the pans for 5 minutes, remove sides of pans and invert onto racks to cool completely. Wrap in plastic and chill.

5. Make the frosting: In a saucepan, combine the cream, butter, corn syrup, cocoa, and salt. Bring to a simmer, whisking. remove from the heat, add the chocolate, and let stand 5 minutes. Add the vanilla and whisk until smooth. Cool to spreading consistency.

6. Halve each cake layer horizontally and sandwich them all with the frosting. Frost the top and sides of the cake. With a round cutter, make "knots" from the muffins, cut off the bottoms of the knots on the diagonal, attach to the sides of the cake, and frost. With the tines of a fork, create patterns to resemble tree bark and tree rings. Decorate with shaved chocolate and dust with confectioners' sugar if desired. Chill, loosely covered, for up to 4 days. Serve at room temperature. Makes 1 cake.

SPICED PLUM GINGERBREAD CAKE

1½ cups water

¼ cup Spiced Plum tea leaves*

½ cup (1 stick) unsalted butter

½ cup firmly packed dark brown sugar

½ cup dark molasses

½ cup dark corn syrup

2½ cups all-purpose flour

1½ teaspoons ground ginger

1½ teaspoons ground cinnamon

½ teaspoon ground cloves

½ teaspoon freshly grated nutmeg

¼ teaspoon salt

2 large eggs

Grated zest of 1 lemon

2 teaspoons baking soda

1 tablespoon fresh lemon juice

4 cups confectioners' sugar

It wouldn't be Christmas without something gingerbread. However, if a candy-bedecked house or icing-coated cookie just isn't your style, consider this sophisticated cake made with spicy plum tea, which gives it a pretty pink color. Thin slices would be a lovely served at an afternoon tea or get-together.

1. Preheat the oven to 350°F. Grease a 10-inch Bundt pan or two 6-inch Bundt pans.

2. In a saucepan, bring the water to a boil. Add the tea, remove from the heat, and steep for 5 minutes. Strain into a bowl, pressing to extract as much liquid as possible.

3. Melt the butter in a saucepan. Stir in the brown sugar, molasses, and corn syrup. Set aside to cool.

4. In a food processor, combine the flour, ginger, cinnamon, cloves, nutmeg, and salt and blend. Add the butter-sugar mixture and blend. Add the eggs and lemon zest and blend until smooth. Transfer to a bowl.

5. Stir the baking soda into 1 cup of the tea; it will bubble up. Stir the mixture into the batter, mixing well, then scrape into the prepared pan. Bake for 40 to 45 minutes for a 10-inch Bundt pan or 20 to 30 minutes for 6-inch Bundt pans. The top should be springy, and a knife inserted near the center should come out clean. Remove the pan and cool on a cake rack.

6. Combine the remaining tea with the lemon juice in a bowl. Sift in the confectioners' sugar, whisking until a thick but spreadable icing is achieved. Pour the icing over the cooled cake and allow it to set before serving. Makes one 10-inch or two 6-inch cakes.

Recipe from Eat Tea *(The Lyons Press), by Joanna Pruess and John Harney.*

*Spiced plum tea is available from Harney & Sons Fine Teas: (888) 427-6398.

CHOCOLATE BRIOCHE LOAF

2½ cups all-purpose flour

⅔ cup Dutch-process cocoa powder

1½ teaspoons baking soda

¾ teaspoon salt

2 large eggs, lightly beaten

1½ cups granulated sugar

6 tablespoons unsalted butter, melted

1 cup sour cream

1 tablespoon espresso powder

1 tablespoon vanilla extract

1 cup dried cherries or cranberries.

1 cup toasted walnuts, coarsely chopped

Confectioners' sugar, for garnish

This light and sweet French bread is made in a regular loaf pan (instead of a brioche mold) for easy slicing. Dried cherries or cranberries provide a tangy surprise. You can make the loaf well in advance of the Christmas bustle, simply wrap in plastic and refrigerate it for up to 5 days. Bring it to room temperature and dust with confectioners' sugar before serving.

1. Preheat the oven to 350°F. Butter a 9- by 5- by 3-inch loaf pan.

2. In a medium bowl, whisk together the flour, cocoa powder, baking soda, and salt. In a large bowl, whisk together the eggs, sugar, butter, sour cream, espresso powder, and vanilla. Add the dry ingredients, a little at a time, stirring until well combined. Fold in the dried cherries and nuts.

3. Transfer the batter to the pan, smoothing the top. Bake for 1 hour, or until a cake tester inserted in the center comes out almost clean (the center should still be a little wet). Let cool in the pan for 10 minutes, then unmold and transfer to a rack to cool completely. Garnish with sifted confectioners' sugar before serving. Makes 1 loaf.

CHOCOLATE CARAMEL TURTLES

60 pecan halves

8 ounces caramels

1 tablespoon heavy cream

6 ounces dark or milk
    chocolate, tempered (see page 127)

Unlike their namesakes, these cute and chewy candies will not be slow to disappear. This recipe uses pecan halves to achieve a turtle shape, but substitute different nuts to your liking.

1. Line a baking sheet with parchment paper. Arrange 12 nut clusters about 2 inches apart on the pan, using 5 pecan halves for each turtle, 1 for the head and 1 for each foot. Leave space in the center of each cluster for the body.

2. In a small saucepan set over medium heat, combine the caramels and heavy cream and heat, stirring until the caramels are just melted. Remove from the heat. With a spoon, fill in the center of each turtle with caramel, leave the outer tips of the nuts uncovered. Spoon the tempered chocolate over the caramel, again being careful to leave the outer tips of the nuts uncovered. Let cool completely until hard; if desired, before completely set, make crosshatch marks with a small knife to resemble turtle shells. Wrap individually in cellophane, and store in a cool place for up to week. Makes 12 turtles.

TEMPERED CHOCOLATE

Tempering, which results in a chemical and physical change in the chocolate, is the process of raising, lowering, and raising again the temperature of melted chocolate. Chocolate in "poor temper" will look dull or gray, or streaked, or have a coarse, granular texture when broken up. Tempered chocolate has a beautifully glossy, crisp texture and will keep longer than untempered chocolate. Use a candy thermometer to check the temperature regularly. Stir the chocolate to make sure your reading is accurate, and hold the thermometer in the chocolate, not resting on the bottom of the pan, which will be hotter. There are several methods for tempering, but the following technique is the most widely used. Be forewarned: It can be quite messy.

1. Break the chocolate into 1-inch pieces or smaller. In the top of a double boiler set over simmering water, melt the chocolate, stirring frequently with a clean, dry spatula, until it registers about 120°F (but no hotter) on a candy thermometer. Remove the double boiler from the heat.

2. Pour two thirds of the chocolate onto a cool, clean, dry surface, such as marble or Formica. With a palette knife, smear the chocolate evenly across the work surface, going back and forth over the chocolate. Bring the chocolate together with a scraper, and use the palette knife to clean the scraper. Repeat the spreading and scraping process, working quickly to prevent lumps from forming, and mixing the chocolate evenly. Check the temperature of the chocolate; when it reaches 80° to 82°F and takes on a dull, matte look, return it to the chocolate in the double boiler. (Depending on the temperature of the kitchen, this process will take anywhere from 5 to 20 minutes of continuous work.)

3. Stir gently and constantly with a rubber spatula, trying not to create air bubbles, until the chocolate is smooth. Take the temperature of the chocolate; it should read 84° to 91°F (dark chocolate should be 86° to 91°F, milk and white chocolate 84° to 86°F). If the chocolate is above 93°F, you will have to begin tempering again from scratch; if it falls below this range, return the pan to the heat to further heat the chocolate.

CHOCOLATE HAZELNUT MADELEINES

1/3 cup all-purpose flour

2 1/2 tablespoons Dutch-process cocoa,
  plus additional for dusting

1/2 teaspoon baking powder

A pinch of salt

2 large eggs

1/3 cup superfine sugar

5 tablespoons unsalted butter, softened

1 tablespoon hazelnut flavoring

1/4 cup very finely ground hazelnuts

Would the addition of cocoa and hazelnut have altered Proust's memory of the madeleine? This sophisticated variation on the traditional shell-shaped miniature cake is an unforgettable accompaniment to a steaming cup of hot chocolate on a cold winter's day.

1. Into a bowl, sift the flour, cocoa, baking powder, and salt.

2. In another bowl, beat the eggs with the sugar until well combined. Beat in the butter and hazelnut flavoring. Fold in the flour mixture and hazelnuts until just combined. Chill, covered with plastic, for 1 hour.

3. Preheat the oven to 375°F. Butter and flour 12 madeleine molds.

4. Divide the batter among the molds, filling them 2/3 full. Bake for 10 to 12 minutes, or until a cake tester inserted in the center comes out clean. Let cool in the pan for 5 minutes, and invert onto racks to cool completely. Before serving, dust with sifted cocoa. Makes 12 madeleines.

DARK CHOCOLATE PEPPERMINT TRUFFLES

2/3 cup heavy cream

1 vanilla bean, split lengthwise

A pinch of salt

8 ounces bittersweet chocolate, melted

1 tablespoon unsalted butter, softened

1/2 teaspoon peppermint oil (available
  at specialty stores), or to taste

1/2 cup Dutch-process cocoa powder

From a cup of hot cocoa stirred with a candy-cane swizzle stick to these tasty truffles, the combination of chocolate and peppermint is a Christmas classic. Make these in large batches to give as gifts or to serve as an after-dinner refresher. The secret to chocolate-free hands when forming the truffles? The chocolate mixture is first frozen, then shaped using two melon ballers before being rolled in cocoa powder.

1. In a saucepan, combine the cream, vanilla, and salt and bring to a simmer. Cool, then scrape the vanilla seeds into the cream and strain into a bowl.

2. In another bowl, combine the chocolate and butter. Stir until smooth. Stir in the cream mixture and peppermint oil. Cover and freeze until firm.

3. Put the cocoa powder into a small bowl. With 2 melon ballers, scoop out a 1-inch ball of chocolate. (Use 1 melon baller to scoop out each chocolate ball and the other to dislodge the chocolate from the first.) Roll the ball in the cocoa powder until completely coated. Continue forming truffles in the same manner. Transfer truffles to a container and chill, covered. These can be prepared 1 week ahead. Makes about 30 truffles.

PEARS POACHED IN RUBY PORT WITH ROSEMARY

1½ cups ruby port

4 cups water

⅔ cup sugar

1 sprig fresh rosemary

12 whole black peppercorns

6 ripe but firm medium pears

These glistening red-tinted sweet pears from Roscoe Betsill, spiced with peppercorns and a hint of fragrant fresh rosemary, are a very special after-dinner presentation served with chunks of blue cheese and toasted walnuts.

1. In a saucepan large enough to hold the six pears, combine the port, water, and the sugar and bring to a boil, stirring to dissolve the sugar. Add the rosemary and peppercorns. Reduce the heat to a simmer.

2. Peel the pears, leaving the stems attached. With an apple corer or paring knife, core the pears from the bottom, leaving the the tops intact.

3. Poach the pears in the simmering port syrup for about 15 minutes, or until tender. Remove from the heat and allow the pears to cool in the syrup. The pears can be kept refrigerated in the syrup for several days. Serves 6.

GRILLED APRICOTS

6 ripe apricots

2 tablespoons fresh lemon juice

3 tablespoons honey

A grating of nutmeg

This simple yet sophisticated dessert from Roscoe Betsill can be made with peaches, plums, or nectarines; orange or thyme flavored honey will give it an extra dimension.

1. Preheat a grill or broiler. Halve and pit the apricots. Toss in a bowl with the lemon juice, honey, and nutmeg. Grill or broil for about five minutes, turning after 3 minutes, until lightly caramelized.

2. Serve with fresh ricotta cheese and sliced semolina raisin bread drizzled with honey. Serves 6.

DOUBLE CHOCOLATE ESPRESSO COOKIES

½ cup all-purpose flour

½ teaspoon baking powder

½ teaspoon salt

½ cup (1 stick) unsalted butter,
softened

⅓ cup granulated sugar

⅓ cup firmly packed light brown sugar

2 large eggs, beaten lightly

1 tablespoon instant espresso powder

1 tablespoon vanilla

8 ounces bittersweet chocolate, melted

1 cup bittersweet chocolate morsels

½ to 1 cup chopped nuts, such as
walnuts or pecans

With a nod to Italian cafe society, these delectable cookies get their extra oomph from espresso. A grown-up interpretation of the classic chocolate chip model, they are the perfect partner for an afternoon latte or cappuccino.

1. Preheat the oven to 350°F. Line two baking sheets with parchment paper.

2. In a bowl, whisk together the flour, baking powder, and salt.

3. In a large bowl, with an electric mixer on medium, cream the butter. Add the sugars a little at a time and beat until light and fluffy. Add the eggs, espresso powder, and vanilla. Reduce the speed to low and add the chocolate. Add the flour mixture a little at a time until blended. Stir in the chocolate morsels and nuts.

4. Drop the batter by rounded tablespoons onto the prepared sheets, spacing the cookies 2 inches apart. Bake for 10 to 12 minutes, or until dry on the outside but still soft in the center. Let cool on the sheets for 5 minutes, and transfer to racks to cool completely. Store in airtight containers for up to 1 week. Makes about 24 cookies.

HAZELNUT GEMS

1 cup (2 sticks) unsalted
   butter, softened

$1/2$ cup confectioners' sugar

$1/4$ teaspoon salt

1 large egg, beaten with 1 tablespoon
   cream

1 teaspoon vanilla

$1 1/3$ cups finely ground toasted
   hazelnuts

$2 1/4$ cups all-purpose flour

1 large egg white, beaten with 1
   teaspoon water for egg glaze

$2/3$ cup jam of choice

An afternoon spent baking Christmas cookies is a tradition for many. While you may already have a lineup of your favorites that friends and family have come to expect year after year, the hazelnuts contribute an adult dimension to these childhood classics and you'll want to add them to your repertoire.

1. In a large bowl with an electric mixer on medium cream the butter. Add the sugar a little at a time and beat until light and fluffy. Beat in the salt, then the egg, a little at a time, and the vanilla. Add $2/3$ cup of the hazelnuts and beat on low just until combined. Beat in the flour until combined.

2. Line two baking sheets with parchment paper. Have the egg white glaze ready and put the remaining nuts in a shallow dish.

3. With lightly greased hands, roll the dough into 1-inch balls. Dip the top half of each ball in the egg glaze and then into the nuts, and arrange the balls about $1 1/2$ inches apart on the baking sheets. With your thumb or index finger, make an indentation in each ball, forming a cavity. Chill the cookies for 30 minutes.

4. Preheat the oven to 325°F. Fill each cavity with a little jam and bake the cookies for 15 to 17 minutes, or until pale golden. Let cool on the baking sheets for 5 minutes, and transfer to racks to cool completely.

5. If the jam needs "topping up," heat additional jam in a saucepan over medium heat until smooth, and add to cookies. Store in airtight containers for up to 1 week. Makes about 40 cookies.

CRANBERRY AND BLOOD ORANGE CONSERVE

2 cups firmly packed light brown sugar

1/2 cup cider vinegar

1 teaspoon ground cinnamon

1/2 teaspoon ground ginger

1/2 teaspoon ground cloves

1 1/2 cups water

1 lemon, zest grated, white pith removed, and fruit cut from between membranes into sections

4 blood oranges, zest grated from 2 oranges, white pith removed from all 4 and fruit cut from between membranes into sections

1 pound cranberries, picked over and rinsed

1 cup dried cranberries, or raisins

1 cup chopped toasted nuts

For those who crave the tantalizingly tart, cranberry and orange is an irresistible combination high in vitamin C. This nut-spiked version of the classic conserve is wonderful served with toast or as a chutney-like relish for roasted goose, turkey, or cold meats. Packed into clear glass jars, the conserve is pretty enough to present as a gift. If you can't find blood oranges, substitute regular oranges.

1. In a large saucepan over medium-high heat, combine the sugar, vinegar, spices, and water. Bring to a boil, stirring, then simmer, stirring until the sugar is dissolved. Add the citrus zests and fruit and simmer 10 minutes more. Add 2 cups of the fresh cranberries and the dried cranberries and simmer, stirring occasionally, for 30 minutes.

2. Stir in the remaining 2 cups cranberries and simmer, stirring occasionally, for 15 minutes. Stir in the nuts. Let cool, then transfer the conserve to sterilized jars, seal with sterilized lids, and process in a water bath for 10 minutes. Cool, tighten the lids, and store in a cool, dark place for up to 1 month. Makes about 4 cups.

CRANBERRY SALSA

1 pound cranberries, picked over and rinsed

1 medium orange, scrubbed, halved, and cut into slices

1/2 to 3/4 medium jalapeño, washed, halved, and seeded

1 cup sugar

2 tablespoons Grand Marnier

The ingredients for this spicy salsa are first frozen, then chilled overnight to allow the flavors to blend. The unexpected, eye-opening combination of cranberries, jalapeno, and Grand Marnier will add zing to a meal featuring the Brine-Cured Roast Turkey on page 112 or other roast poultry or even game.

1. Freeze the cranberries, orange slices, and jalapeño until firm.

2. In a food processor, combine the frozen ingredients and pulse until cut into small pieces. Transfer to a bowl. Stir in the sugar and Grand Marnier. Cover and chill for at least 24 hours or up to 5 days. Makes about 4 cups.

CRANBERRY VINEGAR

1 pound cranberries, picked over and
  rinsed

4 cups rice vinegar

Zest from 1 navel orange,
  removed in strips

A twist of orange peel for garnish

With the season for fresh cranberries so fleeting, it is important to make the most of them. This simple recipe preserves their flavor in an aromatic vinegar that is equally delicious splashed over fresh fruit or used in a vinaigrette.

1. In a bowl, crush the cranberries. Add the vinegar and orange zest, and let stand, loosely covered, in a cool, dark place for 3 days.

2. Strain the vinegar mixture into a saucepan and bring to a boil. Pour into a sterilized decorative bottle and let cool. Add a corkscrew of orange peel to the bottle for garnish. Store in a cool, dark place for up to 3 months. Makes about 4 cups.

HERB VINEGARS

4 shallots, peeled

4 whole cloves

1 quart white wine vinegar

1 teaspoon whole black peppercorns

1 teaspoon sugar

1/2 teaspoon sea salt

FOR HERBS:

3 large sprigs rosemary, 6 large sprigs
  thyme or lemon thyme, or 1 small
  bunch tarragon, plus extra sprigs for
  garnish

Use these vinegars to add subtle herbal flavors to salad dressings or pickles. Or decant them into decorative bottles for gift giving—they look beautiful lined up on a pantry shelf.

1. Stud each shallot with a clove. In a saucepan set over medium-high heat, bring the vinegar to a boil. Pour the vinegar into a sterilized jar and add the shallots, peppercorns, sugar, salt and herb of choice. Let cool. Cover and let stand in a cool, dark place for 2 weeks.

2. Strain the vinegar into a sterilized bottle, add a fresh herb sprig (thyme for thyme vinegar, rosemary for rosemary vinegar, etc.), and seal. Store in a cool, dark place for up to 3 months. Makes 4 cups.

WOODLAND ANGEL

Long pinecone for the body

Acorn for the head

1 milkweed seed pod for the wings

2 pipe cleaners

Golf tee

4 inches of 22 gauge wire for hanging

White spray paint

Hot-glue gun and glue

Craft knife

Scissors

A walk through the woods and fields or a visit to a local nursery can yield a trove of seeds, nuts, leaves, bark, and dried plants that can form the basis of all kinds of decorations and ornaments, from garlands to tiny wreaths. Here we've transformed some woodland findings into angels that soar across the tree boughs and herald the Christmas season. We've painted our angel white, but you can paint yours silver or gold to match the palette of your tree.

1. Wrap 2 or 3 inches of wire around the top of the pinecone, leaving the free end to extend vertically to form a hanger.

2. Hot-glue the nut (head) to the top of the pinecone, positioned as shown in the photo.

3. Separate the two halves of the milkwood pod to use as the wings.

4. Hot-glue the rounded ends of the wings to the nut and the top of the pinecone (with the wire extending between the wings).

5. Wrap the ends of the two pipe cleaners around the throat of the golf tee. Bend the pipe cleaners to form arms. Position the tee on the face and bend the arms toward the neck, trimming the pipe cleaners with scissors to fit. Hot-glue the horn and arms to the face.

6. Spray-paint the angel with several coats of white paint, letting the paint dry between coats.

Variations

Use feathers, dried grasses, or sprigs of pine for the wings. Choose seed pods that have interesting shapes or have fluffy strands still attached. If you can't find a nut the correct size, use a wooden bead for the face. Instead of a horn, fashion a drum or a lyre from other natural materials.

NUT TOPIARY

6 inch bucket or pail

6 inch square of Styrofoam

8-inch Styrofoam ball

2 bags of large nuts, such as walnuts or
chestnuts

2 bags of smaller nuts or seeds, such as
hazelnuts or pumpkin seeds

Spray paint

Hot-glue gun and glue

Craft knife

Although not a true topiary, this easy-to-make decoration is just as versatile. Like a real topiary, it can be formal or completely casual; with a guest's name painted on the container, small versions can serve as placecard holders, larger ones as centerpieces. Use an antique container or a simple terra-cotta pot, or paint a galvanized bucket, as we did here.

1. Spray-paint the outside of the container. Let dry.

2. With the craft knife, shave down the edges of the Styrofoam square until it fits snugly inside the container.

3. Hot glue the Styrofoam ball to the top of the square, let dry, and place in the container.

4. Begin at the bottom edge to hot-glue the large nuts to the surface of the ball. Cover the entire ball as evenly as possible.

5. In the spaces between the large nuts, hot glue the small nuts or seeds. If the spaces between the nuts are very small, you can mount each little nut or seed on a toothpick or short piece of wire and insert into the Styrofoam. You may have to drill a small hole in a nut.

Variations

Add some extra color or texture to your topiary by putting dried flowers or berries between the nuts. You can introduce a whole new palette by soaking seeds in food coloring, laying them out to dry on paper towels, then adding them as accents between the nuts. Or spray-paint your topiary gold or silver.

STOCKING WITH VELVET CUFF

1 yard of print fabric

1 yard of contrasting lining fabric

1/2 yard of velvet

2 yards of cording

12 small gold beads

Rich fabrics trimmed with cording and gold beads transform this simple stocking into an elegant addition for any mantel.

1. Decide on the size of the stocking. Ours is about 18 inches high and 8 inches wide at the cuff. Make a paper pattern that is 1/2-inch larger all around than your planned stocking.

2. Fold the print fabric in half. Place the paper pattern on top. Cut all around the pattern, through both layers of fabric (to yield two stocking shapes). Repeat with the lining fabric.

3. With the right sides of the stocking facing, pin and sew (using a 1/2-inch selvage) from one edge around to the other edge. Repeat with the lining pieces.

4. Turn the stocking right side out. Place the lining inside the stocking so that the wrong sides of the lining and print fabric are facing. Turn a 1/2-inch hem on the stocking top toward the inside. Turn a 1/2-inch hem of the lining to meet the stocking hem. Pin the two seams together and sew all along the top edge.

5. Cut cording to fit along the edge of the stocking and hand-stitch to the seam.

6. To make the velvet cuff, cut a piece of velvet 19 inches by 12 inches. Fold the fabric in half lengthwise with the right sides facing. Sew along the long edge using a 1/2-inch selvage, making a long tube. Turn the tube right side out.

7. Turn one edge of the tube under 1/2 inch and pin. Slip the raw end of the tube into the seamed end and fit the cuff to the top of the stocking. Blind-stitch the pinned seam closed.

8. Slip the cuff over the stocking. Pin into position, aligning the top of the stocking to just below the top of the cuff. Blind-stitch the cuff to the stocking from the inside.

9. Sew on decorative beads to the bottom hem of the cuff.

DÉCOUPAGE GIFT BOX

One 6-inch or 8-inch round cardboard or
   wooden box

Vintage illustrations for the top

Patterned paper for the base and sides

Acrylic medium

Spray paint in the color of your choice

6 inches of ½-inch-wide ribbon

White glue

Scissors

Hand drill with ⅛-inch drill bit

Découpage is an easy way to transform the simplest container, from an old chocolate box to a cardboard box purchased at a crafts store.

1. Spray-paint the inside top and bottom of the box. Let dry. Spray-paint the outside bottom of the box; let dry.

2. Cut out the images you have chosen for the top of the box. You can color-copy the illustrations if you prefer, sizing them up or down as needed. Set aside.

3. Cut a round of paper 1 inch larger than the box top. With the circle centered on the box top, fold the edges of the paper down around the top. Cut small slits in the folded edge at half-inch intervals. Set aside.

4. Brush white glue evenly over the top of the box, and about half an inch down the sides. Position the circle of paper on the glued top. Smooth to remove any trapped air bubbles. Let dry.

5. Cut a length of paper to fit around the side of the box plus a ½ inch for overlap. Coat the underside of the paper with white glue and attach to the box, overlapping where the paper meets. Smooth to remove air bubbles and let dry.

6. Brush the back of each illustration with white glue and position on the box top. Smooth and let dry.

7. Coat the top and sides of the box with acrylic sealer. Let dry.

8. With a craft knife, cut two small half circles (about ½-inch radius) on either side of the bottom edge of the box top. This will make it easier to lift off the top.

9. Drill two ⅛-inch holes spaced about ½ inch apart in the center of the box top. Thread the ribbon through the holes from the inside and tie in a pretty bow on the top of the box.

Variations

Use silver or gold gift wrap, vintage wallpaper, or old Christmas cards to cover the sides of the box, or color-copy old book illustrations. To personalize the box, cover it with copies of Christmas photographs of the person you are giving it to or pictures of their house or garden.

PAPER CONES

Vintage images

Large paper clip

Scissors

1/8-inch hole punch

Hot-glue gun and glue

8 inches of 1/2-inch-wide ribbon

Visions of sugarplums deserve a nostalgic container. Hung from the tree, a garland, or the mantel, these traditional paper cones make charming holders for candies, tiny gifts, or sprigs of greenery. Fashion yours using images from antique cards, gift wrap, magazines, even vintage handkerchiefs.

1. Photocopy your image onto 8- inch by 11-inch card stock. Size the image to fill most of the card.

2. Lay the photocopy image side down on a flat surface. Holding down one corner of the paper (this will be the point of the cone), roll the adjacent corner toward the center. As you form the cone, tighten the twist toward the bottom point and loosen the twist at the top.

3. When you have the shape you want, use a paper clip to hold the twist of the cone in place, then hot-glue along the seam just under the edge.

4. Trim the top of the cone straight across or into whatever shape you desire.

5. Punch a hole in the thickest part of the cone about an inch in from the edge. Fold the ribbon lengthwise, thread the ends through the hole toward the inside, and knot the ribbon several times to secure.

Variations

These cones can be varied in any number of ways. Glue decorative trim such as braid, tinsel, or rickrack to the edge of the cone and add a tassel to the bottom. Coat the cone with acrylic medium and sprinkle with clear glitter. Trim the edge of the cone with pinking shears. Collage last year's family Christmas photos to make a new cone for every year, or if you're using the cone to enclose a gift, use a photo of the recipient.

Gift Bags

1/2 yard fabric

1 yard ribbon

Sewing supplies

Pinking shears

Presented in a luxurious bag, the humblest item becomes very special. You won't need much fabric, so choose glamorous satins or brocades and trim with rich, shimmery ribbons. These instructions are suitable for a bottle of wine or a flavored oil or vinegar, but you can make one any size or shape you like.

1. Using pinking shears (so the fabric won't unravel) cut an 11-inch by 18-inch rectangle from the 1/2 yard of fabric. Cut a circle 6 inches from the diameter from the remaining fabric.

2. Fold the fabric rectangle lengthwise with the right sides facing. Fold the ribbon in half with the right sides facing. Lay the ribbon between the layers of fabric (with the ends extending toward the center) so the folded end is inside the seam about 3 inches from the top edge. Pin along the seam line, making sure the folded end of the ribbon is caught in the seam. Sew the seam using a half-inch selvage.

3. Pin the circle of fabric to the bottom edge of the bag using a half-inch selvage. Sew the seam securely all around.

4. Turn the bag right side out.

5. Hem the top edge by turning 1/4 inch of the fabric toward the inside, then turning another 1/4 inch. Sew along the bottom edge of the seam.

6. Place your gift inside, then tie the ribbon in a bow.

Variations

You can customize your bag with initials. Use machine embroidery or a simple satin stitch to hand-embroider the letters, or use fabric paints or markers together with some small stencils. For a more decorative look, use a contrasting lining fabric, fold over a cuff, and add buttons, beads, or other trims around the top.

Resources

The following is a chapter-by-chapter listing of sources for as many of the items pictured in this book as possible. Every effort has been made to ensure the accuracy of addresses, telephone numbers, and Websites, but these may change prior to or after publication.

INSPIRED BY NATURE

pages 10–17
Shells from She Sells Sea Shells, 1157 Periwinkle Way, Sanibel Island, FL 33957; (239) 472-6991

page 11
Screened garden lanterns from Paris Market Collection, Alda's Forever, www.aldasforever.com

page 12
Compote from English Country Antiques, P.O. Box 1995, Bridgehampton, NY 11932; (631) 537-0606

Shell sphere, papers from Loose Ends, 2065 Madrona Avenue S.E., Salem, OR 97302; (503) 390-2348

Bell Jars from Abigails, 3219 Industrial Street, Alexandria, LA 713301; (800) 678-8485

page 14 (top left)
"Casa Azul" cream soup cup and platter, "Casa Picco" salad plate, "Chambord" dinner plate, "Bernadotte" champagne flute and goblet from Villeroy & Boch, 35 Main Street, Southhampton, NY 11968; (631) 283-7172

page 15
"Alexa" 77-inch sofa in denim from Mitchell Gold, 135 One Comfortable Place, Taylorsville, NC 28681; (800) 789-5401

Shell prints from English Country Antiques, P.O. Box 1995, Bridgehampton, NY 11932; (631) 537-0606

page 16 (top left)
Paper from Loose Ends, 2065 Madrona Avenue SE, Salem, OR 97302; (503)390-2348

Raffia, from Raffit Ribbon, 1155 Shames Drive, Westbury, NY 11590; (516) 333-6778

pages 27
Stockings from Christmas Cove Designs, P.O. Box 128, Richmond, ME 04357; (800) 737-2128; www.christmascovedesigns.com

TOKENS OF JOY

pages 35
Ribbons, boxes, paper from Tail of the Yak, 2632 Ashby Avenue, Berkeley CA 94705; (510) 841-9891

page 37
Stockings from Clover Linen, (770) 266-5713

pages 40-41
Interior design by Stephen Shubel Design Inc., 11 Ross Common Ross, CA 94957; (415) 925-9332

"Taffeta Tabis" from Clarence House, 211 East 58th Street, New York, NY 10022; (800) 632-0076

"Manoir" from Nobilis at Kneedler Fauchere; (415) 861-1011

Toile paper from Prize, 1415 Green Street, San Francisco, CA 94109; (415) 771-7215

Striped/diamond paper from Pine Street Papery, (415) 332-0650

Ribbon from Bell'ochio, 8 Brady Street, San Francisco, CA 94103; (415) 864-4048

Flowers and favors from Verdure, 3014 Benvenue Avenue, Berkeley, CA 94705; (510) 548-7764

page 42
Cones from Paper Dreams, 42 Leonard Road, South Royalton, VT 05068; (402) 664-3077

MAGICAL TOUCHES

pages 52-54
Ornaments from D. Blümchen & Company, P.O. Box 1210, Ridgewood, NJ 07451; (866) 653-9627; www.blumchen.com

pages 55, 56 (bottom)
Flowers and mini-trees from Spruce, 75 Greenwich Street, New York, NY 10014; (212) 414-0588

Cranberry garland from Midwest of Cannon Falls; online catalog, www.midwestofcannonfalls.com

page 56 (top)
Flowers from Belle Fleur, 11 East 22nd

Street, 2nd floor, New York, NY 10010; (212) 254-8703

page 57
Wreath and garland from Surroundings, 224 West 79th Street, New York, NY 10024; (800) 567-7007

Hurricanes from Two's Company, www.twoscompany.com

Birch candles from Zodax, 14040 Arminta Street, Panorama City, CA 91402; (800) 800-3443

page 59
Ornaments from D. Blümchen & Company, P.O. Box 1210, Ridgewood, NJ 07451; (866) 653-9627; www.blumchen.com

page 60
Ornaments from You and Me, 1350 S.W. 92nd Avenue, Owatonna, MN 55060; (507) 451-5381

page 62
Mirrors from Carvers' Guild, P.O. Box 198, West Groton, MA 01472; (978) 448-3063

Ribbon from Hyman Hendler & Sons, 67 W. 38th Street, New York, NY 10018; (212) 840-8393

page 63
Flowers from Belle Fleur, 11 East 22nd Street, 2nd floor, New York, NY 10010; (212) 254-8703

page 67
Wreaths from Armand Wagner L'atelier; 011-33-1-47-00-72-65

KITCHEN HOLIDAY

page 69
Fabric topping honey jars from Osbourne & Little. To the trade only, 979 Third Avenue, Suite 520, New York, NY 10022; (212) 751-3333

page 72 top
Paper from Kate's Paperie, 561 Broadway, New York, NY 10012; 212-941-9816; www.katespaperie.com

page 72 (bottom)
Wallpaper from "Country Life," Waverly. Call for the retailer nearest you: (800) 423-5881

page 74
"Hatbox" tins from Stray Dog imports. To the trade only, 565 McFarland Avenue, Rossville, GA 30741; (866) 478-7297; www.straydogimports.com

page 77
Base from Home Essentials; 3001 Woodbridge Avenue, Edison NJ 08837; (800) 417-6218

HOLIDAY SUPPER

page 78
"Pomfret" candlestick from Simon Pearce, P.O. Box 1, Windsor, VT 05089; (800) 774-5277; www.simonpearce.com

page 81
"Provincial garden" luncheon plate in blue from Spode for Colonial Williamsburg; (800) 446-9240

page 83 (top right)

Dinner plate from Bernardaud;
(800) 884-7775 or (800) 448-8282

Buttons from Tender Buttons,
143 East 62 Street, New York NY
10021; (212) 758-7004

page 83 bottom left

Stationery Lauren McIntosh for Swan
Papel, from Tail of the Yak, 2632
Ashby Avenue, Berkeley,
CA 94705; (510)841-9891

page 84

Compote from Simon Pearce,
"Hartland," PO Box 1, Windsor, VT
05089; (800) 774-5277;
www.simonpearce.com

Platter from Dansk "Wild Willow;
(800) 293-2675;
www.dansk.com

Spoon in compote and fork on platter from
Country Dining Room Antiques, 178
Main Street, Great Barrington, MA
01230; (413) 528-5050

Artel "Narcissus" flutes from Gump's,
135 Post Street, San Francisco, CA
94108; (415) 982-1616

"Quince" place mat from Dransfield
and Ross, available at Bergdorf
Goodman 754 5th Avenue,
New Yok NY 10019;
(212) 753-7300.

page 85 (top)

Soup bowl "Illusion," Barbara Barry
from Haviland; (201) 635-1404
www.haviland-limoges.com

page 85 (bottom)

Charger and salad plate from Country
Dining Room Antiques, 178 Main
Street, Great Barrington, MA 01230;
(413) 528-5050

Pierced creamware tray from Hartley
Greens & Co., Leeds Pottery; P.O.
Box 46, Selby, North Yorkshire
Y085ZR; 044(0)1757 213556
www. leeds-pottery.com

*"English King" fork, salad fork, spoon,
and dessert spoon* from Tiffany & Co.;
(800) 526-0649;
www.tiffany.com

Artel "Narcissus" wineglass and goblet
from Gump's, 135 Post Street,
San Francisco, CA 94108;
(415) 982-1616

Sweets & Desserts

page 92

"Paneled Thistle" glass plates from L.E.
Smith Glass Co., 1900 Liberty Street,
Mount Pleasant, PA 15666;
(800) 537-6484

page 93

Pink place mat from A.B.H.

Scalloped napkin, antique cup and saucers
from Tabletop Design;
(631) 231-1313

page 100

Blue and white "Ciel" china from
Gien, available through Baccarat;
(800) 777-0100

page 101

Crystaflower cake stand from L. E. Smith
Glass Co., 1900 Liberty Street,
Mount Pleasant, PA 15666;
(800) 537-6484

page 102 top

Gold-edge napkins from Dransfield &
Ross, available at Bergdorf Goodman
754 5th Avenue, New Yok NY
10019; (212) 753-7300

"Fern" crystal compote from William
Yeoward Crystal; (800) 818-8484;
www.williamyeowardcrystal.com

page 103

*Dessert plates, spode, mother-of-pearl serving
spoon, and silver basket* from Country
Dining Room Antiques, 178 Main
Street, Great Barrington, MA 01230;
(413) 528-5050

Pierced creamware tray from Hartley
Greens & Co., Leeds Pottery;
www. leeds-pottery.com

Quentin Bacon
pages 78, 79, 80, 81, 87, 93, 95, 98

Jim Bastardo
pages 25, 26, 27, 38 (top), 39, 137

Guy Bouchet
pages 66, 67

Susie Cushner
pages 8, 10–16, 34, 37, 42 (right), 60, 61

Richard Felber
page 65 (bottom right)

Sheeva Fruitman
page 3 (right)

Steve Gross & Sue Daly
pages 22 (top right), 83 (top left)

Bill Holt
pages 2, 3 (left), 33, 35, 40, 41, 43, 83 (bottom left), 138, 144

Charles Maraia
pages 9, 54–57, 63, 72 (right)

Jeff McNamara
pages 18–21, 23 (top and bottom right), 24, 28, 42 (left), 51(right), 52, 53, 59, 65 (top right), 134, 135, 139

Susan Gentry McWhinney
pages 65 (top right), 68, 69, 70, 71, 72 (right), 73–77, 92, 143

Rob Melnychuck
pages 45 (top right), 68, 70

Minh & Wass
pages 65 (bottom left), 88, 89

Steven Mark Needham
page 32

Toshi Otsuki
pages 29 (left), 31 (top right, bottom left, bottom right), 38 (bottom), 48–50, 51(top), 62

David Prince
pages 5, 90, 91, 94

Steven Randazzo
pages 1, 140

Michael Skott
pages 22 (bottom right), 45 (top left, bottom left, bottom right)

William Steele
page 31 (top right)

Ann Stratton
pages 84, 85, 83 (bottom right), 99, 100

Dominique Vorrillon
page 96

Alan Weintraub
pages 36, 136

Michael Weschler
page 97

Marlene Wetherell
pages 46, 47, 83 (top right)